Doing Ethnography Today

Doing Ethnography Today

Theories, Methods, Exercises

Elizabeth Campbell and
Luke Eric Lassiter

WILEY Blackwell

This edition first published 2015
© 2015 Elizabeth Campbell and Luke Eric Lassiter

Registered Office
John Wiley & Sons, Ltd, The Atrium, Southern Gate, Chichester, West Sussex, PO19 8SQ, UK

Editorial Offices
350 Main Street, Malden, MA 02148-5020, USA
9600 Garsington Road, Oxford, OX4 2DQ, UK
The Atrium, Southern Gate, Chichester, West Sussex, PO19 8SQ, UK

For details of our global editorial offices, for customer services, and for information about how to apply for permission to reuse the copyright material in this book please see our website at www.wiley.com/wiley-blackwell.

Library of Congress Cataloging-in-Publication Data applied for

Hardback ISBN   978-1-4051-8648-3
Paperback ISBN   978-1-4051-8647-6

A catalogue record for this book is available from the British Library.

Cover image: © Nik Merkulov / Shutterstock.

Set in 10/12.5 pt MinionPro-Regular by Toppan Best-set Premedia Limited

Printed in the UK

For Rosalie

Contents

Preface   x

1   Introduction: Conceptualizing Ethnography   1

Ethnography is as Personal as it Gets   4

Ethnography is Collaborative   5

Ethnography is Hermeneutic   6

Ethnography is Creative and Constitutive   7

Ethnography Grapples with the Idea of Culture, however Deeply
Compromised   8

Ethnography is Mostly Art   8

Exercise – Taking Stock: Exploring your Limits and Possibilities   10

Suggested Readings   13

Suggested Websites   14

2   Fields of Collaboration   15

The Field Today   19

On the Actual Complexities of Collaboration   21

Exercise – Engaging Collaborators and Creating
Research Questions   24

Suggested Readings   26

Suggested Websites   27

3 Emergent Design   **30**

Exercise – Intentional Reciprocity   32

Uncertainty and the Collaborative Process   34

Ethics and Ethical Commitments   36

Exercise – Developing Project Codes of Ethics   39

Recognition or Anonymity?   40

Exercise – Ethics, IRBs, and Other Subjects   41

Issues of Authority: Ethnographer as Facilitator,
Research Participant as Counterpart   44

Exercise – Revisiting Project Limits and Possibilities   46

Suggested Readings   47

Suggested Websites   48

**4 Engagement: Participant Observation and
Observant Participation**   **50**

Exercise – One Scene, Many Positions   54

Participation   56

Interlude: Equipment Check   61

From Participant Observation to Observant Participation   64

Fieldnotes: From Definitions, Meanings, and Practices
to Storied Observations   66

Exercise – Developing Your Own (Fieldnotes) Style   69

On Fieldnote Forms   72

Exercise – Writing With   75

By Way of Conclusion… 77

Suggested Readings 80

Suggested Websites 80

5 Interviews and Conversations **84**

Living with Interviews 87

Exercise – Issues for Interviews 89

The Changing Nature of Interviews 94

Exercise – Interviews as Conversations 97

Interviews (and Conversations) in Ethnographic Research 98

Exercise – Talking about Transcripts 104

Suggested Readings 108

Suggested Websites 109

6 Inscriptions: On Writing Ethnography **113**

Exercise – Making Sense of Materials 116

"What is Ethnography?" Redux: On the Emergence of Contemporary
Ethnographic Forms 120

Exercise – Writing Ethnography 126

Toward Collaborative Writing and Transformation 129

Exercise – Collaborative Writing 131

Suggested Readings 134

Suggested Websites 135

Index 138

Preface

This book is the outgrowth of a conversation on ethnography we began 20 years ago at the University of North Carolina at Chapel Hill. We were graduate students back then – Beth in folklore and Eric in anthropology – and we were taking a seminar entitled, "The Art of Ethnography," which emphasized the craft's humanistic and artful possibilities. Although we have both worked in a variety of settings and conducted numerous ethnographic and other projects since then, we keep coming back to that conversation, and we continue to view the craft of ethnography as an artful, humanistic form in search of meaning, connection, and, above all, change.

When we were coming of age as ethnographers, feminist, postmodernist, and other critical scholars were furiously interrogating, theorizing, and reconstituting ethnography along these lines. It was an exciting time. It was also an incredibly challenging time because it required us to both think about and do research in new and very different ways. The theories and methods of feminist, postmodernist, and other critical theorists – particularly those that concerned dialogic and collaborative theories and methods – changed not just how ethnography is conducted or written, but how its goals and purposes are constituted. Those theories and methods heavily influenced our work as students, and continued theoretical developments in these areas influenced our work as professionals as we started our careers in Folklore and Anthropology, respectively. We document many of the ethnographic projects we conducted within this framework in the pages that follow, but one project, in particular, radically transformed how we viewed the possibilities of collaboratively researched and written ethnographies to change people, their relationships with one another, and even communities.

That was the Other Side of Middletown project, and it is, in many ways, responsible for much of what we have written since, including this book. We will have a lot more to say about the Other Side of Middletown (as well as other projects) in the pages that follow, but we should elaborate on this a bit here. When we lived in Muncie, Indiana (1996 to 2004) – Beth working for a range of local arts and history organizations and Eric for Ball State University – we had the unique opportunity and privilege to develop, along with others, a community-university collaborative ethnographic project that eventually came to involve over 75 people, including faculty, students, and African American and other Muncie community members. Much of the work we did in that project mirrored other ethnographic work we had done before in other settings, such as when ethnographers and community members design research questions together, conduct research collectively, or co-interpret and co-create written ethnographies. But this particular project worked on us in ways that we had never experienced before, at least at this level. The very intense processes of faculty, students, and community members researching and, especially, writing together changed all of us to varying degrees, some in profound ways. The intense collaborative processes that worked across differences in race, class, community, university – among a host of other things – foregrounded not just the project, but many other collaborative actions that grew out of the project. (For more on this, see chapter 2, especially the notes, which include several references to articles that document these developments.)

Many ethnographers, of course, have described similar processes, and how ethnographic fieldwork can involve us in different kinds of collaborative relationships and actions, and thus produce change. So in that regard there was nothing particularly unique about the experience. But for us, it was the quintessential collaborative ethnographic project, one that brought research, pedagogy, university, and community into the same stream, and in ways that powerfully articulated the promises of the dialogic and collaborative ethnography we had learned about as graduate students and sought to practice in our professional work. Importantly, however, it also inspired in us a new appreciation for how the intersubjective and dialogic processes of co-researching and co-writing ethnography itself could be mobilized as a form of public dialogue and exchange to inspire changes in human relationships.

We have written in several places about how the project changed the trajectory of our thinking about ethnography along these lines (again, see the notes in chapter 2 for references). As we have detailed in many of those reflections, the project raised several new problems and issues for us, too. While we were completing the project, for instance, Eric began to wonder (and read) about similar kinds of projects, their histories, and what kind of possibilities lay ahead for doing these kinds of collaborative ethnography (e.g., how they might transform anthropological pedagogies), work that eventually prompted his *Chicago Guide to Collaborative Ethnography*.

Beth began to think more and more about the creative and constitutive possibilities of writing together, and soon after we moved to West Virginia in 2005, she decided to pursue another degree in English composition, rooting her dissertation research in the possibilities for collaborative writing that she had so powerfully witnessed while serving as the editor for the Other Side of Middletown project. (In fact, her dissertation, "Being and Writing with Others," begins with the Other Side of Middletown project.)

Twenty years after Chapel Hill, and 10 years after publication of *The Other Side of Middletown*, we are now working primarily with graduate students in education and in the humanities and navigating a broad array of interdisciplinary and collaborative research projects including but not limited to ethnography. We are still talking about the transformative possibilities for ethnography we first explored as graduate students and experienced so powerfully in the Muncie project, and about the still unfolding possibilities for ethnography as collaborative, creative, and constitutive; as an agent of change; and as artful, humanistic, and hermeneutic. This book, then, is an extension of that conversation. But it also joins up with another conversation, which now involves us in discussions with our current students who come to ethnography, on the one hand, from quantitative, qualitative, or mixed methods backgrounds (in the case of our education students) or, on the other hand, from the arts, cultural, historical, or literary studies (in the case of our humanities students). So we also wrote this book with these students in mind, as an open letter of sorts, so that they might have a better understanding of where we are coming from and what we are up to (and what we hope they might try to do).

We have thus written this book primarily for advanced undergraduate and beginning graduate students (and similar audiences) working in a variety of fields – from those who might like to think about and do ethnography outside of familiar quantitative–qualitative dichotomies to those who might want to expand their readings of society and culture into realms of ethnographic research. But we have also written this book for students and others who want to engage ethnography at a time when many of the promises of ethnography, theorized when we were graduate students, are simultaneously being more fully realized in practice "in the field," even as they are being overshadowed by the increasing dominance of STEM-infused views of science in our universities.

We should point out that we do not view this book as exhaustive, and that we have not written it to be a traditional stand-alone or step-by-step manual or guide. Our purpose here has been different. What we want to offer is more food for thought than any model, or standardized set of methods. Although we strongly believe that doing and writing ethnography can never be a one-size-fits-all affair, we also believe that one can learn a set of contemporary concepts and ideas around which ethnography is built, and upon which to found one's own application and interpretation of ethnography. This book, then, is meant to cultivate experience in ethnographic fieldwork, reading, and writing that emphasizes both theoretical and methodological direction for doing ethnography today.

We begin chapter 1, the book's introduction, by outlining some of the key assumptions behind our approach to ethnography as well as our approach to this text. These include several of the themes already mentioned: that ethnography is personal as well as collaborative; hermeneutic, creative, constitutive, and artful; and oriented toward dynamic and complex ideas of culture and society. In chapters 2 and 3, "Fields of Collaboration" and "Emergent Design," respectively, we explore how contemporary collaborative contexts for doing ethnographic fieldwork today – which include but are not limited to the moral and ethical commitments between and among those engaged in collaborative research – provide the contours through which ethnography is built and sustained, and touch on how research design can emanate from this collaborative process.

In chapter 4, "Engagement: Participant Observation and Observant Participation," we highlight ethnographic processes of participation, observation, and documentation and take up the art of "observant participation"; we also explore the processes of crafting fieldnotes within this context. In chapter 5, "Interviews and Conversations," we take up the ethnographic interview and consider how field conversations materialize within the context of dialogic and collaborative ethnographic work. And finally, in chapter 6, "Inscriptions: On Writing Ethnography," we explore the process of ethnographic writing itself (broadly defined), including its organization and continuing interpretation as well as the actual process of composing ethnographic texts. This section of the book also includes a discussion on various modes of dissemination past and present, including the process of creating different kinds of collaborative ethnography through dialogue, co-interpretation, and co-inscription. Each chapter, we should mention, is followed by a list of "Suggested Readings" and "Suggested Websites," which offer additional resources on subjects covered.

In addition to brief theoretical discussions about particular issues, we have included Exercises throughout. These Exercises, we should note, are meant to engage readers in practice as they read. Although most begin with an explicative or theoretical discussion followed by a set of recommended activities, readers will quickly observe that the Exercises do not all follow a single, set form. The lengths of the introductory discussions vary, and the activities' substances and processes are often quite different; again, this is not a conventional step-by-step guide to doing ethnography. We have drawn heavily on our own training and experience to design these Exercises and organized them in a way that follows the (more or less) customary evolution (in our experience) of an ethnographic project. Because writing and dialogue are critical to contemporary ethnographic processes, nearly all of the Exercises rely, at least to some degree, on the production of private or shared texts, and on partnered, small-group, or large-group discussions.

*****

Many people have contributed to our ongoing conversation about ethnography, collaboration, and possibility that serves as the impetus for this book. Former professors, colleagues, friends, and the various ethnographic collaborators with whom we have worked have helped to shape many of the ideas we explore here. They include Rachel Bruenlin, Theresa Carter, Elizabeth Chiseri-Strater, Sam Cook, Graham Crow, Clyde Ellis, Les Field, Carolyn Fluehr-Loban, Hurley Goodall, Glenn Hinson, Billy Evans Horse, Susan Hyatt, Michelle Johnson, Seth Kahn, Ralph Kotay, Charles Menzies, Danieala Nieto, Gian Pagnucci, Lee Papa, Joanne Rappaport, Celeste Ray, Helen Regis, Linda Spatig, Bonnie Sunstein, Joe Trimmer, and Bob White. Any failures to articulate their eloquent ideas are entirely our own, of course. Speaking of which, a very thorough and insightful set of reviews written by a very thoughtful group of reviewers improved this book markedly. And finally, we need to single out an old friend.

Yet another outgrowth of the Other Side of Middletown project has been our continued relationship with Rosalie Robertson, who was the Senior Editor at AltaMira Press when we set about finding a publisher for the book. Rosalie (who had worked with Eric on a previous book project) immediately became intrigued with the idea and engaged AltaMira Press as a collaborative partner throughout the entire process from beginning to end. Soon after the completion of *The Other Side of Middletown*, and after Rosalie had moved to Wiley Blackwell, we began discussing writing this book. We were supposed to have it to her by 2010. It did not happen. But Rosalie stuck with us (and commented on more than a few drafts) and we are deeply grateful for her faith in us. Although she is no longer with Wiley Blackwell, we dedicate this work to her.

Elizabeth Campbell and Luke Eric Lassiter
March, 2014

Chapter 1

Introduction: Conceptualizing Ethnography

Ethnography is traditionally described as both a fieldwork method and an approach to writing. As fieldworkers, ethnographers participate in the lives of others, observing and documenting people and events, taking detailed fieldnotes, conducting interviews, and the like. As writers, ethnographers organize, interpret, and inscribe this collected and, as many argue, constructed information as text. Over the last century or so, ethnography's fieldwork and writing have come to signal very particular sets of assumptions, epistemologies, and expectations, and to yield recognizable – some might say, predictable – textual forms.

Though its histories and methodologies mix elements of both the sciences and the arts and their histories, ethnography also inhabits very particular ways of being, by which we mean ways of encountering, thinking about, interpreting, and acting in the world around us. Ethnographers often identify as and talk about "being ethnographers," and although they may argue about whether what they do is science or art or both, most would agree that being ethnographers changes how we think, how we interact with others, and even how we move through the world. It does so because it brings us directly into contact with diverse people leading varying ways of life. Ethnomusicologist Nicole Beaudry points out that doing ethnographic

Doing Ethnography Today: Theories, Methods, Exercises, First Edition. Elizabeth Campbell and Luke Eric Lassiter.
© 2015 Elizabeth Campbell and Luke Eric Lassiter. Published 2015 by John Wiley & Sons, Ltd.

fieldwork "remains a challenging experience because it teaches us that there are many different ways for human beings to be themselves."[1]

What Beaudry says of ethnographic fieldwork has certainly been the case for us. Between us, we have done various kinds and differing levels of ethnographic work, all of which have brought us into contact with many different kinds of people. We have worked with K-12 math and science teachers, activists and community organizers, and descendants of a pre-Civil War plantation in West Virginia; African American pioneer descendants, black Civil War re-enactors, "Middletown" residents, and state and county fair participants in Indiana; Waldensians, tobacco farmers, and Lumbee Indians in North Carolina; recovering addicts, historic preservationists, and bikers in the urban South; students and faculty in a university-based digital technologies center; tradition bearers in rural Kentucky; and Kiowa Indians in southwestern Oklahoma. We have written fieldnotes and conducted interviews; recorded songs and taken photographs; traced maps (physical as well as social); dug into national, state, and local archives; documented folk culture and traditions; organized focus groups; collected life histories; participated in a whole host of activities; and, of course, produced ethnographic reports that have ranged from academic ethnographies to performance pieces to museum exhibits to briefs for state agencies. Though our fieldwork methods have generated a wide range of recognizably ethnographic products, they have also consistently led to other outcomes, often unexpected, for us and for the diverse people with whom we have worked, from educational programs, to National Register nominations, to political action, to other applied, and often activist, work.

The processes of doing fieldwork, producing texts, and connecting to unexpected – and not always directly related – outcomes have both challenged and changed us, sometimes in profound ways. Ethnography, when done with the experiential and intellectual depth it deserves, brings us face-to-face with our own assumptions and ethnocentrisms. As we study with and learn from others – who often seem very unlike ourselves – we are pushed to move beyond understanding and toward transformation. Our own ethnographic work has fundamentally shifted our understandings of what it means to be, for instance, a biker, an addict, or a Kiowa singer, and in bringing about those shifts, has also affected how we relate to others and, for that matter, to ourselves. Some projects forced us to examine how we may have stereotyped or over-generalized the experiences of some people. Other projects have forced us to think about class or race or gender in new ways. And still others have led us to navigate relationships differently. For example, an ethnographic project on bikers that Beth did as a folklore graduate student unexpectedly healed a rift that had long existed between her and one of her sisters. Although family therapy had not been a goal at the outset of that project, being with bikers – and talking with them, and writing about them, and sharing emerging understandings with them – brought the very different worlds she and her sister then lived in closer together. That proximity led both to imagine, and then to create, different ways of being together.

Such experience is not at all unusual when it comes to doing ethnography. In an ethnographic study of a small Iowa community where he grew up, anthropologist Douglas Foley describes in *The Heartland Chronicles* how a complex matrix of relationships between and among whites and Mesquaki Indians yield multi-layered ethnic and racial negotiations through time. But he also describes how the processes of ethnographic fieldwork helped him understand his own experiences and memories growing up in the town, and of how the process of "one person trying to understand him- or herself enough to understand other people" can lead us to understand others and our relations with them better. In Foley's case, he was led to learn more about his father (whom he never met) and make connections with his mother (who helped shape his views of Indians from an early age) that he had not made before, which, in turn, helped him understand on a deeper level the subject of his study. He writes, for example, that "knowing Mom better was absolutely crucial for understanding abandoned Mesquaki mothers and grieving Mesquaki men." Importantly, though, Foley points out that the process of ethnographic fieldwork and cross-cultural understanding "takes much more than simple empathy. It takes endless hours of listening to people and observing, constant recording and reflecting, a grab-bag of theories to ply. But knowing yourself always seems like the biggest part of understanding others."[2]

As Foley suggests, knowing yourself as you come to know others is a big part of "being an ethnographer." But as Foley also suggests, so is learning to be with – and listen to and take seriously – others. It should not come as a surprise, then, that many ethnographers doing ethnography today emphasize more than a purely methodological approach, calling attention instead to ethnography's histories, philosophies, epistemologies, and ontologies. Although learning the "how to's" of ethnographic fieldwork and writing are necessary for doing ethnographic work, actually "being an ethnographer" requires us to reach beyond method. Consider, for example, this quotation from the late communication studies scholar and ethnographer, H. L. "Bud" Goodall:

> [T]he choice of "being an ethnographer" is a profound philosophical commitment that very much transcends ordinary concerns about the utility of fieldwork methods or even prose styles. Not everyone is suited for this line of work. Unlike traditional methods of social science, ethnography is not theory-driven, method-bound, or formulaic in its research report. Ethnography requires a person who is comfortable living with contingencies, who is good at associating with others from widely diverse backgrounds and interests, and who likes to write. As such, ethnography is more of a calling than a career, and the decision to do it – as well as the ability to do it well – seems to require more of a particular, identifiable, but oddly ineffable attitude toward living and working than belief in method.[3]

Not everyone may see ethnography as a kind of "calling." But everyone should, at the very least, understand that ethnographic practice requires commitments that are different from other research approaches. One of the most important of these is committing to a particular *way of being with people*, which brings up an important consideration for any student of ethnography, regardless of whether or not you are invested in "being an ethnographer" as such: in spite of its many different approaches (and there are many), at the end of the day, *doing and writing ethnography is about engaging in, wrestling with, and being committed to the human relationships around which ethnography ultimately revolves.* Folklorist Carl Lindahl, whose home discipline is rooted in the processes and relationships of ethnographic fieldwork, has this to say: "I regularly tell students on the verge of their first foray into fieldwork that folklore, done as it should be, is as personal as it gets: fieldwork can easily double the number of birthday cards you send and funerals you attend."[4] To Lindahl's statement – with which we absolutely concur – we add this: the relationships that emerge "in the field" are as rewarding and challenging and "real" as any others, especially because they encourage us to know others as well as ourselves. Understanding that ethnography will necessarily expand and complicate your own personal web of relationships is, we think, a very important place to start in conceptualizing ethnography.

*****

This book is grounded in the idea that ethnography begins and ends with people. Ethnography, as we understand and practice it, articulates a very particular way of being that foregrounds the personal and relational; assumes an underlying collaborative perspective; necessarily implicates an interpretive and hermeneutic approach; works within the realm of the cultural; and depends on the very human arts of understanding. To elaborate exactly what we mean by all of this, in the sections below we briefly outline some of the basic assumptions we bring to the practice of ethnography and thus to this book. We think you should know what we are up to right up front.

Ethnography is as Personal as it Gets

As Lindahl says so poetically, engaging the complexities of fieldwork also means engaging the complexities of human relationships. Those relationships, of course, are framed by the dynamics of experience, through which we participate in people's lives and engage them in dialogue. To be open to this process is to be open to experience itself, to its often unanticipated twists and turns, and to the unexpected places it may take us. We see experience as an apt metaphor for the ever-emergent qualities of both ethnographic fieldwork and ethnographic writing. But more than this, we also see experience and the human relationships it generates as the crucial and vital space within which the contours of ethnographic practice – from its design to its composition – are negotiated. As such, we see the processes of doing ethnography as deeply personal and "positioned" activities. This implicates a complex intersection of worldviews, sensibilities, agendas, hopes, and aspirations that are an inevitable part of each individual endeavor, and of every relationship into which an individual may insert her- or himself, including the relationships that constitute ethnography.

If, as we believe, doing ethnography is deeply personal and positioned, then it is also deeply subjective. In this sense, we adhere to a long tradition of philosophical and critical thought that scrutinizes (and is skeptical of) the very idea of objectivity, and that considers the pursuit of a purely objective point of view a misdirected foray. In our view, ethnography proceeds not from an objective, or even reasonably objective, research position – an idea which we believe masks rather than erases one's worldviews, sensibilities, agendas, hopes, and aspirations. Rather, ethnography develops out of an unambiguous consideration of one's own experiences, positions, and subjectivities as they meet the experiences, positions, and subjectivities of others. In this way, ethnographic practice is a relationship-based intersubjective practice that demands honest and rigorous appraisals of our own assumptions and ethnocentrisms as we learn about those of our ethnographic collaborators through co-experience and shared dialogue.

Ethnography is Collaborative

Ethnography has always depended, at least to some extent, on collaboration. Indeed, it would be hard to imagine any ethnographic project without at least some level of shared work. But collaboration in ethnography has most often been limited to fieldwork processes. In the field, for example, ethnographers work closely and talk deeply with key "informants" or "consultants," collaboratively constructing and interpreting cultural concepts, practices, and so on. Writing up the "results" of these dialogic collaborations, however, has traditionally been left to the ethnographer, and control over the final work (and often its dissemination) usually remains in her or his hands. This kind of collaboration tends to begin and end in the field; it is more a collection method or strategy than an underlying perspective or philosophy for doing and writing ethnography.

We do want to say that there can be good reasons for carrying out ethnography like this. We have written ethnographic reports for local community groups, for instance, who have requested this kind of arrangement. But we also want to say that, in our view, ethnography is at its best when collaboration carries through from beginning to end. Taking seriously the human relationships that give rise to collaborative processes means that we also take seriously the ethical and moral commitments we make to ourselves and others as our ethnographic projects unfold. This can and often does extend well beyond the mechanics of fieldwork: the obligations and responsibilities of collaboration can animate the entire process of an ethnographic project, from its conceptualization, to its design, to its inscription. If we are open to it, that is.

In the context of this manuscript, then, we assume a stance of collaborative ethnography, which strives for – even if it does not always fully attain – ongoing collaboration at every point in the development of an ethnographic project. The ethnography we have in mind is responsive to the commitments established between and among ethnographers and the people with whom we work, and it shares authority and control whenever and wherever possible. Ethnographic practice undertaken in this way can be controversial, even today; students (and, to some extent, junior scholars) should be aware that not all who identify as ethnographers are willing to enact or support this particular kind of ethnography.

Ethnography is Hermeneutic

We view ethnography as hermeneutic, in that we believe it is an entirely and inescapably interpretive affair. Of course, it has long been assumed that fieldwork involves the reading, interpretation, and production of cultural "texts" (human actions, expressions, and traditions, for example), and that writing ethnography is intimately tied to this dynamic and dialogic process. Doing and writing ethnography involves us in more than just the analysis of texts, however. It is also intimately tied to the personal: as we participate in others' lives and engage them in dialogue, we cannot help but be influenced by the unfolding and ongoing co-experience that develops among us. This co-experience, moreover, changes our subjectivities, and as those subjectivities change, our positions – our ways of being in and interpreting the world around us – move into states of flux. This is a basic fact of ethnography: as we learn about others, we learn about ourselves; as we learn about ourselves, we learn anew about others; and when we are open to what we learn about others and ourselves, we change.

This is not, we want to emphasize, a one-way street; the processes of learning and transformation are by no means limited to the ethnographer. In collaborative ethnography, in particular, where both ethnographers and their "interlocutors" or "consultants" struggle together to co-interpret and even co-theorize experience via the ethnographic text, the process can be multi-directional and multi-transformational (as when collaborative ethnography prompts collaborative actions). We take for granted that this co-learning process can (and often does) transcend both ethnographic method and ethnographic product. In fact, learning from and with each other can be, in our minds, one of the most important things we do as ethnographers; it can be (and often is) much more significant than any field method we might acquire or any monograph we may write.

Having said this, though, we do view the ethnographic monograph and the ongoing discussions about ethnographic theory and practice as key to doing and writing ethnography, and indeed, to learning how to "be an ethnographer." The regular and ongoing engagement with actual texts – *independent of any individual ethnographic project or partnership* – is absolutely critical to honing an interpretive stance for doing and writing ethnography, and is thus central to ethnographic practice. Being an ethnographer, or even just learning the basics of ethnographic method, requires a firm commitment to the activity of *reading* (a lot) and interpreting text as ongoing intellectual practice, intellectual practice that ideally prompts complex understandings of the complicated settings in which we do ethnography. "Being an ethnographer" requires "being a reader"; broad and deep reading will ideally absorb us in the vast range of ethnographic possibilities we can then draw upon when doing our own ethnographic work. (For this reason, we offer a short list of written ethnographies and other sources at the end of each chapter that we find particularly useful and interesting.) We assume, then, that this hermeneutic activity is as crucial to ethnography as fieldwork and that without regular and reflective *reading* ethnography becomes a very thin endeavor indeed.

Ethnography is Creative and Constitutive

Along these same lines, we also assume, as Goodall point outs, that whatever final form ethnography may take, writing (in whatever form it may take) is intimately tied to this hermeneutic process. And as such, we assume that ethnography is inherently creative and constitutive: creative and constitutive in the sense that engaging in the activity of writing is not just about putting already formed thoughts and ideas down on paper or up on the screen. The processes of writing itself also *generate*, *interpret*, and *transform* thoughts and ideas; those thoughts and ideas, in turn, have the potential to *change the way we think* about things, and thus *how we navigate the world* in which we live. Scholars of literacy have known, for a very long time, that reading and writing, on their own, have this extraordinary potential. But when we view collaborative ethnographic writing through the lens of creative and constitutive action, we see that the activity of inscription takes on another layer of possibility that engages us in collective thinking, reflection, action, and transformation. This particular aspect of ethnography is enormously exciting and, as yet, it remains largely untapped; for these reasons, it is also one of this book's animating precepts.

Ethnography Grapples with the Idea of Culture, however Deeply Compromised

The notion that learned systems of meaning (ideas, behaviors, practices – in a word, culture) inform human experience to a greater extent than does our biology has been central to the idea of ethnography since its inception. Ethnographers in the late nineteenth and early twentieth centuries, for example, provided descriptions of culture as alternatives to biologically determined (and in many cases, overtly racist and sexist) descriptions of exotic and seemingly strange human behaviors. In this light, culture became an extremely powerful concept for elaborating how and why humans around the globe constructed their worlds in such vastly different ways. Indeed, the tremendous variety of human experiences and expressions like language, marriage customs, child-rearing practices, funeral rites, religion – just to name a few – made much more sense when viewed through the lens of culture.

But culture is an enigma now, a problematic concept for many scholars. It was once widely accepted that cultural systems were separate and bounded; today, we know that has never been the case. We know that cultural ideas, behaviors, and practices overlap, and that quintessentially authentic or pure traditions have never existed, not even in the days of "lost tribes" and other imagined isolations. Anthropologists, for instance, no longer speak of the actuality of individual "cultures"; they speak instead of multiple and interdependent cultural – and political, economic, and social – systems. These systems are informed and shaped by complex and intersecting histories that surface in the present as complicated and intertwined global processes.

Some theorists, who see culture as an irredeemably outdated concept, have gone so far as to suggest that we abandon the idea of culture altogether. While we agree that older concepts of culture still in use today can be problematic, we also believe, as historian James Clifford once put it, that "culture is a deeply comprised idea [we] cannot yet do without."[5] Indeed, the idea of culture remains a powerful concept for apprehending the deeper meanings of human activities, complex and interconnected as they are, especially when juxtaposed with increasingly popular contemporary explanations that (like their nineteenth-century and early twentieth-century counterparts) reduce human behavior to biological – especially genetic – processes. In many ways, ethnographers, who work in the realm of the cultural, offer a particular and unique perspective on the human condition that mercifully resists reduction and over-simplification.

Ethnography is Mostly Art

In that ethnography assumes a primarily hermeneutic stance; that it requires the writing and interpretation of texts engaged on multiple levels; that it is deeply personal, dialogic, and collaborative; and that it grapples with the idea of culture, we view ethnography to be an intellectual pursuit in the best tradition of the humanities. Because we also view it as having the potential to transform ourselves, others, and even the communities in which we live and work, we believe that ethnography asks us to fully engage the human arts of understanding, and that it can thus be an act of peace (however modest or small) in a world wrought with *mis*understanding, conflict, and violence. Collaborative ethnography, in particular, emphasizes finding common ground on which to build co-understandings and co-actions (without eschewing difference) instead of producing rarified texts that may put ethnographic outcomes in direct tension, and even conflict, with the people with whom we work. Doing and writing the kind of ethnography we have been describing should, ideally, provide space for the open and reciprocal exploration of ideas. Crafting those ideas into artful ethnographic forms, in turn, can connect us with each other, with our communities, and, ultimately, with broader understandings about what it means to be human in all of our complexities.

We thus couch ethnography more within the arts (particularly of participation, conversation, and inscription) than within the sciences. Contemporary ethnography does connect to a long tradition of systematic and empirical methods based in experience (as generated by fieldwork, for example), which in turn have stemmed from scientific assumptions about the acquisition of knowledge (that all is, in theory, knowable, for example), and the problem-solving potential of applying that knowledge to larger human issues (as in comparative sociology, for example). Ethnography as art, in our view, is not necessarily opposed to science, but it is different from science. And it seems to us that when ethnography is positioned as a kind of "objective," scientific research method that can be acquired and applied independent of its humanistic, textual, and intellectual histories and traditions, its promise is limited (in the same way that, say, the history, function, and meaning of Shakespeare and the theatrical arts are limited when reduced to method).

In many academic circles, ethnography is often situated within the larger field of qualitative methods, and often sits opposite quantitative methods on a continuum of positivist, scientific inquiry. This paradigm is also limited, in that it too often reduces ethnographic and other qualitative approaches to techniques for supplementing quantitatively generated data (as in many "mixed methods" models). In these cases, ethnographic and other qualitative inquiry turn out to be little more than diluted quantitative inquiry (as when a single open question is added to a survey, for example), or as a source of illustrations for the more "serious" quantitative work (as when heartwarming scenes or compelling quotations are sprinkled throughout a report). When the very complex work of describing, navigating, and interpreting human relationships is reduced in this way, it is easy to see why qualitative work is so often construed – and constructed – as inferior to quantitatively generated data.

Although we recognize that, for many, ethnography draws from and informs discussions of both qualitative and quantitative theories and methods, we insist that, ultimately, conceptualizing ethnography must stand outside that positivist continuum, and resist the restraints that limit its full range of possibilities. Ethnography, in its practice, certainly does mix a wide range of research methods – from drawing maps to doing surveys to taking photographs. But in the end, ethnography is humanistic inquiry: an artful form that, as anthropologist Clifford Geertz once famously wrote, provides the curious, "sociological mind with bodied stuff on which to feed."[6] As such, ethnography is ultimately about exploring the greater truths of what it means to be human in ways that positivist inquiry, whether posed in either qualitative or quantitative schema, simply does not address. Ethnography, like any other artful form, is more meaning-full, and has much more to offer us when it stands on its own, when each ethnographic project is evaluated according to its own unique potential and possibility. We are thus philosophically and epistemologically suspicious of the idea that learning how to do and write ethnography can be reduced to mastering a method or instrument that can be applied in the same or similar ways across settings. Again, although learning different methods and approaches is essential to learning the craft (and we do explore those methods and approaches in all of the chapters that follow), ethnography is, in the end, more complicated than this. Ethnography necessitates epistemological rigor *and* ontological flexibility. It asks us to be persistently creative, imaginative, and original. And it demands, most importantly, that we become comfortable with the contingencies and ambiguities of human relationships.

EXERCISE – TAKING STOCK: EXPLORING YOUR LIMITS AND POSSIBILITIES

Ethnography is, at base, a fundamentally personal, social, and situated enterprise. The specific projects you engage will necessarily draw upon your own *experiences and ethnocentrisms*, the socio-cultural problems and possibilities that are available to you, the institutional contexts within which you find yourselves, the resources you can tap, and so on. We believe that before you actually make any decisions or commitments about your project and partners, you must think intentionally and deeply about your own – and your group's, if you are working that way – full range of possibilities.

When we were students at UNC-Chapel Hill (Eric was working towards a PhD in Anthropology and Beth towards an MA in Folklore), we took a seminar with folklorist Glenn Hinson called "The Art of Ethnography." The seminar very effectively merged theory and practice: over the course of the semester we simultaneously carried out experimental ethnographies and met weekly to discuss important contemporary readings and issues, as well as the progress of our own projects. One of the discussions we both remember well asked us to honestly consider what kinds of groups we could reasonably expect ourselves to work with. For those who had been trained to think of social science in more positivistic terms, that seemed a rather startling discussion topic. Many were accustomed to much more traditional research frames, where the "value" of potential knowledge rather than the subjectivities or preferences of the researchers drives decisions about whether or not to engage particular groups and/or questions.

But contemporary and collaborative ethnographic practice is different – we believe that it almost has to be different – because it asks us to seek open, reciprocal, and productive interactions and relationships with other human beings (in all of our complicated and problematic glory). In the seminar that day, we talked passionately about whether or not we could work – openly, honestly, and collaboratively – with hate groups, or religious fundamentalists, or human traffickers, or the uber-rich. We also argued about whether or not we *should* work with such groups. Clearly, such studies would yield important and quite necessary knowledge. But if our frame for ethnography asserted that building understanding was as important as building knowledge, we had to ask ourselves if – setting aside the not insignificant problem of gaining access to such groups – we could honestly try to build understanding with Klan members, for example, or with those who committed "honor" killings. Some of us asked if we should even try to understand those positions, or if some things were simply beyond the pale. Others insisted that ethnography could not pick and choose, and that ethnographers should be open to all potential subjects. (We want to say here that this was a tremendously interesting and passionate conversation, one we *highly* recommend that you and your fellow researchers and collaborators also take up.) In the end, few of us could imagine – for reasons of preference, ideology, class, gender, experience, and a host of others – being able to engage in honest, respectful, or reciprocal relationships with such groups.

Of course, we have named extremes here, but wrestling with those extremes does illuminate the kind of honest personal appraisal any collaborative project demands. As you begin thinking about and planning your own projects, remember that ethnography necessarily asks us to engage actual, living people whose experiences could be either familiar or foreign to us, whose opinions we might share or abhor, and whose agendas we may or may not be able to embrace. And so it is critical that you begin your ethnographic work by thinking about, exploring, and discussing the experiences, preferences, and prejudices you carry with you.

This exercise will ask you to do just that; first on your own, then in collaboration with a partner, then in discussion with the larger group.

1. On your own, write about the experiences, preferences, and prejudices you bring with you to this project. This writing will be completely private; no one will see it but you. We grant that acknowledging, naming, and describing your preferences and prejudices is an intimidating task, but you can start addressing it by answering specific questions like these:
    -   How does your background (religious, cultural, ethnic, regional, family, class, and so on) predispose you toward (or against) particular people, groups, or practices?
    -   List several potential ethnographic projects you'd like to undertake. Why do they interest you? What ties them together? List several you would not consider under any circumstances. Why do you feel that way?
    -   Describe your social skills. What situations do you thrive in? What kinds of situations do you find intimidating (or dull, or intolerable, or …)?
    -   Are there certain kinds of situations – physical, cultural, or otherwise – that may be difficult or dangerous for you to navigate?

    Follow whatever leads these questions open, and be as honest as you can with yourself. Again, this part of the exercise is private and will not be shared.
2. Revise and condense your responses down to a page or two that you feel comfortable sharing with someone. Select a partner, then share this condensed response with her or him. He or she will also share his or her responses with you.
3. Read and discuss each other's responses. Feel free to ask follow-up questions, and to seek clarification when you are not sure of something. Take notes.
    -   Where do your experiences, preferences, and prejudices intersect? Where do they diverge?
    -   Where has your partner drawn hard and fast lines? Where is there room for negotiation?
    -   What is most interesting or surprising about your partner's responses? What is most interesting about your reactions to each other's responses?
4. Share the notes you have just taken with each other. Separate to fully read each other's notes, then come back together to discuss them. How well did your notes capture your discussion? What did you find particularly

interesting about each other? How did each of you write about the things that were difficult, or unflattering? If significant gaps remain in how you understand each other's possibilities and limits, make time for additional discussion. By the end of this discussion, you should be able to talk for a few minutes about your partner's background and experience, and about what kind of a project your partner would be best suited to and why.

5. Come together as a whole, and have each person spend a few minutes reporting on her partner. The partner being discussed should remain silent as she is being discussed, but may offer corrections and/or additional details after her partner has finished.

When you are working as part of a group, it is also important to have open discussions about where the interests of group members converge and diverge, and the degree to which your different positions are set or flexible. Using a process similar to what is outlined above, build a group discussion that leads to an understanding of what the group's possibilities and limits are. In addition to the valuable information and critical "reality checks" these kinds of discussions provide, the intentional process of openly sharing and negotiating these issues also serves as important experience in collaboration and with collaborative processes.

Suggested Readings

Barz, Gregory F., and Timothy J. Cooley, eds. 2008. *Shadows in the Field: New Perspectives for Fieldwork in Ethnomusicology*, 2nd ed. Oxford: Oxford University Press. This collection features essays on the contemporary challenges of conducting fieldwork and ethnography in the field of ethnomusicology.

Behar, Ruth. 1996. *The Vulnerable Observer: Anthropology that Breaks Your Heart*. Boston: Beacon Press. A personal account that eloquently combines ethnography and personal memoir.

Denzin, Norman K., and Yvonna S. Lincoln, eds. 2013. *The Landscape of Qualitative Research*, 4th ed. London: Sage. A collection of essays on qualitative research that provides a broad range of perspectives for thinking about the concepts and issues that inform doing ethnography and closely related research today.

Geertz, Clifford. 1973. *The Interpretation of Cultures*. New York: Basic Books. A classic collection that every student of ethnography should read, especially its most well-known essay, "Thick Description: Toward an Interpretive Theory of Culture." Geertz famously (and almost single-handedly) shifted ethnography's orientation from one focused on positivism and deduction to one focused on interpretation and meaning.

Suggested Websites

Engaged Ethnography – http://engagedethnography.wikispaces.com/ Provides information about ethnographies that explicitly encourage social, political, and other forms of change.

Side by Side – Practices in Collaborative Ethnography – www.sidebyside.net.au/ A blog about the intersections of art, ethnography, and collaboration. The site has several interesting posts about collaborative art and ethnography that use "creative methods (such as photography, video, writing, visual art) to represent community and cultural stories in a collaborative way."

Notes

1. Nicole Beaudry, "The Challenges of Human Relations in Ethnographic Enquiry: Examples from Arctic and Subarctic Fieldwork," in *Shadows in the Field: New Perspectives for Fieldwork in Ethnomusicology*, edited by Gregory F. Barz and Timothy J. Cooley (Oxford: Oxford University Press, 1997), 63–83.
2. Douglas E. Foley, *The Heartland Chronicles* (Philadelphia: University of Pennsylvania Press, 1995), 220.
3. H. L. Goodall, Jr, in James A. Anderson and H. L. Goodall, Jr, "Probing the Body Ethnographic: From an Anatomy of Inquiry to a Poetics of Expression," in *Building Communication Theories: A Socio/Cultural Approach*, edited by Fred L. Casmir (Hillsdale, NJ: Lawrence Erlbaum Associates, Inc., 1994), 100.
4. Carl Lindahl, "Afterword," *Journal of Folklore Research* 41, nos. 2/3 (2004): 173.
5. James Clifford, *The Predicament of Culture: Twentieth-Century Ethnography, Literature, and Art* (Cambridge: Harvard University Press, 1988), 10.
6. Clifford Geertz, *The Interpretation of Cultures* (New York: Basic Books, 1973), 23.

Chapter 2

Fields of Collaboration

Throughout this book, we will refer back to the Other Side of Middletown project, one of the most rewarding experiences we have ever had as ethnographers. The project brought more than 75 students, faculty, and members of a local community together to collaboratively research and write *The Other Side of Middletown*, a book that aimed to address the absence of African American history and experience in the scholarly and popular literature on Muncie, Indiana.

Muncie, or "Middletown," as it became more widely known, was made famous in the 1920s and 1930s by the publication of Robert and Helen Merrell Lynd's *Middletown* (1929) and *Middletown in Transition* (1937). In the decades that followed those two texts, Muncie became a research destination for scholars from around the world. To this day, in fact, scholars continue to visit Muncie, and to research and write about what has become one of America's most studied small cities. Until very recently, however, the city's black population had been virtually absent from this constantly expanding body of literature, even though at the time of the Lynds' study, there were proportionately more African Americans in Muncie than in major cities like Chicago and New York.[1]

The Other Side of Middletown project surfaced into a stream of other projects involving African Americans in and around the Muncie region, several of which

Doing Ethnography Today: Theories, Methods, Exercises, First Edition. Elizabeth Campbell and Luke Eric Lassiter.

Beth, in particular, had been facilitating through her work at a local museum and cultural center. One of those projects was a collaboratively researched and developed museum exhibit on early nineteenth-century African American pioneers in east central Indiana, which engaged modern-day black farmers and other living pioneer descendants in the exhibit's design, direction, and production. Several members of Muncie's African American community were closely involved in that project, and in other projects that emerged as the exhibit evolved into other iterations across local and state levels. Some of those projects included a photography exhibit on black Muncie, a theatrical production on race relations, and, eventually, the Other Side of Middletown project.

Closely involved in each of these projects was Hurley Goodall,[2] a former firefighter, union leader, and Indiana State Legislator who had dedicated his retirement to local history and activism. We learned through the course of working on the African American pioneers exhibit that he had spent many years working – through oral history, archival research, and political action – to rectify the very conspicuous absence of African Americans from Muncie's historical literature. In *The Other Side of Middletown*, and in several more recent articles, we offer this background in some detail; suffice it say here that the absence of African Americans from the Middletown literature both disturbed Hurley Goodall and compelled him to action.[3]

In the original Middletown studies, the Lynds set out to document and explain the massive changes that modernity was bringing to American communities. Though they warned regularly and specifically against casting Muncie as typical of American experience (in fact, as they took pains to point out, early twentieth-century Muncie was actually quite atypical), the Lynds' works – and, most likely, the pseudonym "Middletown" they chose for Muncie – had the effect of defining Muncie as the middle American place. And because the Lynds had chosen not to include Muncie's African Americans in their original study, the norm for that quintessentially middle American place ended up being constructed, from the very beginning, as almost entirely white. For Hurley, the Middletown literature, which had come to represent "typical America" for so many, had thus effectively removed "black experience" from "typically American" experience.

As we got to know Hurley, we became increasingly intrigued by his work and allied ourselves with his commitment to "set the record straight." After some initial exploratory discussions between Eric and Hurley about writing a collaborative ethnography on Muncie's black community, the three of us began to talk about the possibility of doing an ethnographic project that would expand to involve an even larger collaboration of students, faculty, and community members. Our first serious meeting about the project took place one evening in Hurley's home office, an entire basement-level floor populated by file cabinets of various heights, colors, and vintages; tables upon which were layered books, folders, photographs, maps, and other documents; an enormous oak desk with neatly organized stacks of incoming and outgoing correspondence; and, next to the desk and in pride of place, a typing desk upon which stood Hurley's trusty IBM Selectric. We drank coffee (and beer) and talked late into that night about what the project might look like: about how we might involve community members as advisors, set up research teams of both black and white students, create different levels of community review, incorporate Hurley's ongoing documentary work, locate other previous work, and find project funding, among many other things. We raised, explored, embraced, and discarded lots of possibilities that night. But there was one thing about which Hurley remained absolutely adamant: we had to publish our work, ideally as a book that would find its way into the Middletown literature as a corrective to Muncie's whitewashing. As he would many more times throughout the project, Hurley told a story about working with a prior group of researchers who, in the 1980s, had received a sizeable federal grant to do a study of Muncie's black community. He worked with the group for over a year, convincing many in Muncie to work with the researchers, including his own mother, who was then in her late eighties. Despite all of the time, energy, and personal capital he expended to help the research team, they never published their results. Hurley was, to put it mildly, more than a little disappointed. Understandably, he was also more than a little reluctant to begin another major project without some sort of assurance that, this time, his efforts would not be in vain. We promised him that although we could not guarantee that our work would be published, we could guarantee him that we would produce a complete and finished text and that we would do our very best to seek out an interested publisher before we even started the project.[4]

To make a rather long and involved story short, we published *The Other Side of Middletown* a little less than four years after that first meeting. The project itself, as is often the case, turned out to be much more than what we originally imagined. Many more people became involved than we initially assumed, for example, and the students (all undergraduates with the exception of one graduate student) did much more work (collecting, for instance, over 150 hours of interviews) than we actually thought possible in the course of a single semester (the spring of 2003, when the bulk of the book's actual research and writing took place).

It is tempting to think that everyone's hard work, tenacity, and dedication were what led to the book's eventual realization. All of those things were certainly factors, but the truth is that we were able to complete the work in such a short time period, and with so many people involved, because of significant project funding and equally significant institutional support, both of which allowed and encouraged the project to unfold in the very particular and unusual way that it did.

The project's major funding came from Ball State University's Virginia B. Ball Center for Creative Inquiry (VBC), a very rare facility that grants faculty and students an entire semester, free of other academic commitments, to work with community partners on a single, common project. Students receive a full semester's worth of credit for the project, faculty are released from other teaching and administrative commitments, and participating communities (and/or community members) are compensated for their time and expertise. The VBC expends considerable resources creating the conditions within which student-faculty-community teams can co-investigate a common problem and then plan and execute a product-based goal or solution: VBC groups have co-produced plays, books, movies, documentaries, and other award-winning products (see, for example, http://www.bsu.edu/vbc). In no small part because of this extraordinary commitment and support, facilitating the Other Side of Middletown project was an incredibly unusual opportunity for us. In fact, we have since come to realize that the two of us are unlikely to experience such an opportunity again in our careers, especially because that level of financial, institutional, and philosophical support for collaborative, immersive, and processual learning experiences is increasingly rare to nearly nonexistent in most of the contemporary academy.[5]

In exchange for that support, the VBC established very particular and rigorous requirements – as they do for all of their projects – demanding the involvement of undergraduate students as creative agents, the participation of community groups as authentic partners, and the active and ongoing interdisciplinary cooperation of academic disciplines and departments.[6] These particular conditions and expectations for collaboration helped to shape the particular form the project, and the book, would eventually take. That undergraduate students from broad interdisciplinary backgrounds would have the opportunity to research and write the majority of the book turned out to be a major component of our own project's particular arrangement. The very deep involvements of community collaborators like Hurley Goodall and others, who, obviously, also had very particular conditions and expectations for the collaboration, were equally important.

Although the particulars of *The Other Side of Middletown*'s final form may be unusual, the project's emergent character – and the intersection of different conditions and expectations for collaboration on the part of Goodall, the VBC, and others – is not. Many of the issues that shaped this project – ideas about and hopes for collaboration, ethical agreements between participants, issues of funding, and the emergence of situated and particular kinds of research design – shape other ethnographic projects as well, albeit in different ways and to varying degrees.

*****

Because so much of contemporary ethnography is characterized by such simultaneous similarities and differences, we want to turn now to a brief exploration of the contemporary field in which most ethnographers do their fieldwork today. In what follows, we consider how current ideas and assumptions about collaboration often position this work; distinguish between perceived and actual collaborative practice; take up issues of emergent research design; delve into the ethical streams through which ethnographic projects are often navigated; and discuss issues of position and authority. We also touch on more practical matters like beginning an ethnographic project, developing research questions, and working with Institutional Review Boards. Thinking about and preparing for fieldwork with these things in mind is a critically important part of the planning that must now go into almost any kind of ethnographic work.

The Field Today

Just as we did in the Other Side of Middletown project, contemporary ethnographers often find themselves stepping into streams of already existing (or prior) projects and partnerships; increasingly, they also encounter explicitly expressed conditions and expectations for collaboration itself that exert considerable influence on the circumstances of most modern fieldwork.[7] Though ethnographic fieldwork has always depended on collaboration – ethnographers have always had to work with others, at least on some level, in order to do ethnography – the contemporary field is suffused with layers of ideas and assumptions about collaboration, much more than it had been in the past. Anthropologist George E. Marcus, writing about anthropologists doing ethnography today, puts it this way:

> [T]here are pressures on fieldwork, coming from multiple directions today, to define itself in terms of the modality of collaboration. Anthropologists confront the "other" (now "counterpart") in the expectation of collaboration, and in their appeal for funds, etc., in their relation to dominating patron institutions, they should represent themselves as collaborators or themselves organized in collaborations. This is all very different from the way in which collaboration has been embedded, neglected, and redeemed in the traditional practice of ethnography. Collaboration instead is a key trope for condensing a whole complex of new challenges.... [8]

One of the most important aspects of preparing for the challenges of modern fieldwork, then, is planning for a field saturated with various and multiple ideas, assumptions, expectations, and hopes for collaboration (i.e., working together in a common effort or project) on the part of ethnographers themselves, the collaborators with whom they work, and the people and institutions that in most cases make ethnographic work possible (employers and funders, for example). These ideas, assumptions, expectations, and hopes may get expressed metaphorically, but they are more and more often set forth, explicitly and deliberately, as organizing and ongoing conditions for ethnographic work. (Think of the VBC funding requirements we described earlier, for example, which established explicit and specific expectations for collaboration.) Just as we did in the Other Side of Middletown project, contemporary ethnographers regularly find themselves working with individuals and groups (consultants, organizational heads, bureaucrats, clients, funders, and so forth) who are also working with, negotiating, and navigating various notions of collaboration. These notions, of course, can be and often are very different from those an ethnographer might have in mind when a project is initially conceptualized and planned.

Whether working abroad or at home, with marginalized populations or with cultural elites, the "field" for which we prepare to do ethnographic work is also becoming increasingly difficult to delineate and define. "The field," or more precisely, "the fields," into which we settle ourselves can no longer be imagined as clearly separate domains of activity, populated by "informants" who live within bounded cultural systems distinct from one's own. Moreover, they can also no longer be positioned as "out there," in separate, "faraway places," as was the custom in classic ethnographies. The fact of contemporary globalization should make all of this absolutely clear. The fields for ethnographic work are now within reach, and they are all around us. In this sense, fields are multi-sited; they are situated not so much in distinct places as in multiple, layered, and often overlapping collaborations.[9] And, importantly, these multi- "sites of collaboration" are often in material tension with one another, as when different collaborating groups with similar interests compete for similar resources or toward different ends. Even when aims and ends apparently coalesce, they are always and invariably internally positioned within complex *research imaginaries* (i.e., how different participants differently imagine the enactments and outcomes of research), which ascribe how different people assume collaboration "should work" in the context of very specific fields of encounter, research, and (inter)action.[10]

To a certain extent, such conditions and imaginaries have always been present in ethnographic work.[11] But in the arenas of research in which contemporary ethnographers now find themselves, ignoring or side-stepping the larger tropes of collaboration and the research imaginaries those tropes engender is, more and more often, simply not possible. It is important to understand that it has not always been this way. Take, for example, Native American studies, an area in which Eric has worked for over 20 years. There was a time – albeit, before his – when ethnographers and other social scientists could settle in a community, pick a few key informants or consultants with whom to work, do their observations and interviews, then write up their studies in relative solitude, often away from that community. Some ethnographers did choose to work very closely with their consultants, collaboratively producing exceptional life histories, song recordings, and even collaborative ethnographies.[12] But back then, this was something ethnographers could choose to either do or not do. Not so anymore: by the time Eric started researching song traditions in southwestern Oklahoma's Kiowa community in the late eighties and early nineties, the Kiowa people with whom he worked expected full and transparent collaboration. And more: collaboration was established – quite clearly – as a condition for both his research *and* his writing.[13] Such expectations are the rule rather than the exception for researchers working in Native communities today.[14] Although this condition may represent ideas, assumptions – and, to be sure, expectations – for collaboration that are very specific to the histories of Native North American ethnography, it also describes the expectations for collaboration we encountered in the Other Side of Middletown project, which are becoming increasingly common in ethnographic work.

On the Actual Complexities of Collaboration

Once we appreciate that collaboration is an organizing trope for much of contemporary ethnographic work – and that it is often explicitly and deliberately centralized as such via complex and overlapping research imaginaries – we must turn to another critically important aspect of preparation for ethnographic fieldwork. Collaboration can seem, on the surface, as simple and agreeable as "working together." But it is far more complicated than this. If we are to collaborate in meaningful ways, we must appreciate, from the outset, the difference between, on the one hand, deeply ingrained perceptions about what collaboration is, and on the other hand, the complexities of how collaboration actually works (or can work) between and among people in practice. Many often naively assume, for example, that agreeing to work with others in a common effort necessarily means that agreement and interpretive accord should characterize the collaborative process throughout. In practice, however, understanding and working with *difference* is critical to successfully working within the context of the actual collaborative partnerships ethnographers regularly encounter, seek out, and cultivate.

As an example of this tension between perceived and actual practice, we offer an applied ethnographic study in which we were contracted to conduct a three-year, in-depth survey of the collaborations between universities, outreach professors, local teachers, and school districts. These university-school collaborations were considered central to the success of a larger federally funded initiative intended to strengthen math and science education in West Virginia (via the ongoing professional development of math and science teachers). Throughout the study, we explored questions concerning, among other things, how the various partners involved in this process understood collaboration itself, how they envisioned their roles in that collaboration, how shifting and competing agendas affected the overall project and its objectives, and how the larger federally funded partnership could be sustained so as to help support and augment math and science instruction in the future. The study was meant to seek understandings about the partnership through time (which we documented in periodic reports); importantly, it was also intended (as we were charged in the first place) to serve as a kind of applied action research, meant to help shape collaborative practice between and among project partners as their collaborative work unfolded.

The project turned into a very interesting collaborative study about collaboration itself. Participants' ideas and assumptions about collaboration – and we refer to our own ideas and assumptions here as well – added another layer of complexity, especially because "collaboration" was particularly critical to how the project's university-school partnerships were "supposed" to work. The larger project placed intense pressures on participating school districts, teachers, and higher education partners to chart meaningful collaborations; indeed, the establishment of sustainable collaborative actions and partnerships was considered central to its success. But different partners had very different understandings of their role in that collaboration. And, as in any collaboration, different partners accepted differing levels of commitment that ranged from "thin" to "thick." That, in turn, created differing understandings of the collaboration that underlined the larger project. Teachers and partnering outreach professors, for instance, articulated the deepest levels of commitment and enacted the thickest levels of participation, as one might perhaps expect. Interestingly, however, the particular histories of different teacher/professor relationships and their commitments to one another (and to their students), led to outcomes very particular to those relationships, outcomes that resisted the pressures of the larger federally funded project to conceptualize and deploy collaboration in ways that could be modeled from one school district to the next. And more interestingly still, the core idea that we would (or could) produce a replicable model for school/university collaboration turned into another kind of trope that, effectively, glossed how collaboration actually works and, ultimately, created confusion among the project's participants.

In this instance collaboration was, from the outset, perceived as something that could work in distinctly instrumental and modeled terms, which could then, it was hoped, be reproduced in other school districts. Of course, that kind of expectation for collaboration, in the end, circumvents how people actually work together on a common collaborative effort or project. Perhaps for obvious reasons, collaboration does not "model" very well from one partnership to the next. In reality, when we enter into collaborations with specific individuals or groups, we begin by making personal decisions to engage in certain kinds of efforts and relationships and not others. Those decisions, of course, intersect with other choices, motivations, circumstances, and possibilities, all of which are wrapped up in, to name only a few variables, previous experience and background, particular situations, personal sensibilities, and individual aspirations.

All of this becomes all the more complicated in the context of doing ethnographic research, where we enter into projects and partnerships that ask us to negotiate our own personal choices, motivations, and sensibilities with those of other people with whom we may choose (or agree) to work. Most such projects and partnerships begin with the assumption that "working together in a joint intellectual effort" is a good thing. But beginning and sticking with such an agreement does not in any way preclude variations in experience and interpretation, or differences in opinion, and disagreement – or even outright conflict – as a project unfolds. Anyone who has ever engaged in any serious collaboration – ethnographic or otherwise – knows that such differences surface regularly and often; arguably, differences are an elemental condition of all human interactions, including collaboration. As most anyone who does collaborative work also knows, such points of contention are rife with both possibility and peril; they have the potential to either strengthen or weaken the relationships that constitute the collaboration, create either productive or counterproductive tension, and either enrich the overall collaboration or lead to its demise.

In the Other Side of Middletown project, for example, various kinds of differences materialized throughout the project. One we regularly encountered concerned how to interpret and then represent different historical events. As one might expect, students, faculty, and community partners often thought differently about what a particular event might mean. Whose interpretation, then, would be presented? How would we decide? What stories, in the end, would the finished ethnography tell? These were just some of the more pointed questions we faced. But we saw these questions and the differences they called up as an extremely positive thing, something that could potentially strengthen the project rather than weaken it. And in the end, we believe that it did. Though the process was never perfect, we spent much time talking about these questions, finding common ground, and, in the end, acknowledging and incorporating our differences in background, experience, and expertise into new stories and into the ethnography itself. Because many who were involved in the Other Side of Middletown project were also deeply committed to our larger goal of completing the project and the text, they were willing to work through differences in ways that helped to strengthen the project considerably.[15]

This is a relatively brief example, but the point is that whenever we engage in forms of collaboration – and this especially includes doing ethnography today – we engage ourselves in interactions that are difficult for many people, especially as they require us to genuinely share control, make concessions, work with others, negotiate ideas and outcomes, labor through (without eschewing) differences, and – perhaps more than anything else – willingly yield to a process that may unfold in ways completely different from what we originally anticipate. This brings us to the emergent contexts within which ethnographers now do ethnographic work, to which we will turn in the next chapter.

EXERCISE – ENGAGING COLLABORATORS AND CREATING RESEARCH QUESTIONS

Once you work out your own personal – and, by extension, group – possibilities, you can turn to the social and cultural possibilities within which you find yourselves. What is available to you? And by that, we mean not just what is possible, or what is interesting, or what is accessible, but what has been done before? What are the research traditions of your particular context? What can you build upon? What should you avoid?

In a place we once lived – a place not known for its ethnic, cultural, or religious diversity – the city's synagogue began objecting to university students who wanted to observe and/or do studies there. The students were not intentionally disrespectful or disruptive, but the congregation was small and services were beginning to have more observers than participants. Moreover, some members had grown weary of their perceived exoticism, especially after more than 100 years in the community.

It is difficult, sometimes, for ethnographers to think outside the frame of exoticism (an exoticism that is always perceived and positional, rather than inherent or essential). But there is a very good reason for this: exoticism was one of ethnography's most powerful foundational narrative frameworks. For classical ethnographers, the convention was to seek distance and difference, to leap out of one's own milieu and land in the middle of a strange world.

Although the idea of a more or less compulsory relationship between ethnography, distance, and difference has been remarkably persistent, it is no longer as uncritically embraced or enacted as it once was. It is not at all unusual today to find project opportunities closer to home, in groups, people, places, and issues with which ethnographers may already share some connection. Project possibilities also emerge out of issues or problems identified by local people; in fact, the best (in our minds) contemporary approaches to ethnography – especially those allied with Action Research (AR) and Participatory Action Research (PAR) – ask ethnographers to begin with the issues and problems that local groups and communities have identified as important. If your aim is to do collaborative work, there is no better place to start than with an issue, problem, or concern to which people have already committed themselves.

1. In small groups, begin to investigate what kinds of ethnographic projects have already been done. There are a number of different avenues to

explore here. Your instructor, facilitator, or organization may have existing projects and/or relationships you might join. If you are working in a university environment, you will find many disciplines and departments that regularly use ethnography and which may also have existing projects or contacts. Anthropology, folklore, education, and sociology, of course, come immediately to mind but many other disciplinary research traditions make regular use of ethnography as well: nursing, business, English, counseling, and criminal justice, to name just a few. Once you have identified who is doing ethnography, use questions and discussions to get a sense of what they are doing. Are there topics or groups that are used very often? Very rarely? Are there past projects that have gone particularly well or badly? (Do not overlook this. What others have done before you can profoundly influence the success of your own project.)

2. Once you have a sense of what has been done, use paired and group discussions to begin deciding what you might do. Keep in mind that collaborative ethnography, by definition, begins in many different ways. Although ethnographers can certainly initiate projects, the best collaborative projects seem to come to ethnographers, rather than from them, and seem to unfold within established relationships or partnerships. Have any groups stepped forward with identified issues or expressed desires for partnership? Do you belong to an organization or community that is confronting particular issues or problems? Look for possible partners and issues in service learning offices, non-profit organizations, social clubs, hobby or interest groups, voluntary organizations, political parties, social service agencies, unions, churches, or businesses. This business of getting started can be very difficult, but do not get discouraged. You will have to summon your imagination and gather your courage! Once issues and organizations have been identified, begin discussions with the people connected to those issues or organizations about what you might want to explore together.[16]

3. Using a process like the one that helped you to identify your own interests, begin negotiating with your partners the larger themes and issues around which you will organize your project. Once you have settled on themes and issues, use them to develop your research questions, which we define as the large, overarching questions or problems that drive your project. Bear in mind that research questions and interview questions are very different: research questions frame the larger project, its overall aims and issues. Interview questions, which are specifically targeted and narrowly focused, dig into the particulars of the research questions.

4. Pay attention to these conversations, and take good notes. When opportunities to share your notes with project participants arise, share them. And follow that sharing with further conversations around how people respond to your notes. After some initial one-on-one and small-group conversations have taken place, we have found that bringing together all of a project's participants is a great way to "officially" begin.[17] When we get to this stage – where willing participants, general issues, and broad questions have been identified – we like to have a "kick off" meeting in which we ask people to introduce themselves, give a bit of personal background, and talk about why they are interested in participating. Then we introduce the larger issues, and work as a group to begin honing project questions and goals. It is important to remember – and to remind others – that these questions and goals can shift throughout the project, but that is part of the collaborative process as well. (In addition to all of the important information the group gathers at this first meeting, we have found that it also serves as a kind of "commitment ceremony" to both the group and the project which begins to strengthen the relationships upon which the project will depend.)

In collaborative research, it seems to us, the best research questions emerge in the negotiation between our own interests, those of our collaborators, and those we encounter in the literature. In the case of *The Other Side of Middletown*, for example (and here we reference both book and project), the university team brought interests related (among other things) to research, history, and service; the community team brought interests related (again, among other things) to experience, justice, and engagement; and the literature brought interests related to Middletown (as an object of study), black history, and ethnographic practice. Although this combination of positions made for occasionally difficult conversations, negotiating those difficulties helped to strengthen the developing collaboration.

Suggested Readings

Bray, John N., Joyce Lee, Linda L. Smith, and Lyle Yorks. 2000. *Collaborative Inquiry in Practice: Action, Reflection, and Making Meaning*. London: Sage. A group of education doctoral students embark on a study of the processes of collaborative inquiry, between and among themselves and with their research interlocutors.

Faubion, James D., and George E. Marcus, eds. 2009. *Fieldwork is Not What it Used to Be: Learning Anthropology's Method in a Time of Transition*. Ithaca: Cornell University Press.

Explores the shifting fields of collaboration in which anthropologists and other ethnographers work today.

Field, Les W. 2008. *Abalone Tales: Collaborative Explorations of Sovereignty and Identity in Native California*. Durham: Duke University Press. An exemplary example of collaborative ethnography that illustrates how the former divisions between "the researcher" and "the researched" are much less clear today. Several of Field's collaborators contribute text and analysis as well as offer emergent co-interpretations of the role and meaning of Abalone in Native California.

Lassiter, Luke Eric, Hurley Goodall, Elizabeth Campbell, and Michelle Natasya Johnson, eds. 2004. *The Other Side of Middletown: Exploring Muncie's African American Community*. Walnut Creek, CA: AltaMira Press. Collaborative ethnography written by an interdisciplinary group of faculty and students with local community members of Muncie, Indiana.

Suggested Websites

University of California, Irvine Center for Ethnography – www.ethnography.uci.edu/ Explores ongoing developments in how "ethnography is conducted, reported, received, and taught," including those dealing with shifting contexts for thinking about and doing collaborative ethnographic research.

Neighborhood of Saturdays – http://neighorhoodofsaturdays.com/ Details a collaborative ethnographic project on an Indianapolis multi-ethnic community carried out by a group of anthropology students under the direction of Dr Susan Brin Hyatt at Indiana University-Purdue University Indianapolis.

The Virginia B. Ball Center for Creative Inquiry – http://www.bsu.edu/vbc Sponsor of the Other Side of Middletown project, the site features a short documentary of the project (see http://www.bsu.edu/vbcarchive/sem_20022003_sprg_lassiter/video/framesetter .html): the full version of the documentary, *Middletown Redux*, is available from AltaMira Press. The site also features several other creative and collaborative projects carried out by Ball State University faculty and students under the auspices of the Center.

Notes

1. For a recent survey on the history of Middletown studies that includes several of the issues concerning the Middletown literature we take up below, see James J. Connolly, ed., "Seventy Five Years of Middletown," Special Issue of the *Indiana Magazine of History* 101, no. 3 (2005).
2. "Hurley Goodall" is not a particularly common name and so it is odd that we would have two different ones in this text, but we do want to point out that Muncie's "Hurley

Goodall" and Communications Studies scholar "Hurley Goodall" are not the same person.

3. For more on the Other Side of Middletown project, see Luke Eric Lassiter, Hurley Goodall, Elizabeth Campbell, Michelle Natasya Johnson, eds., *The Other Side of Middletown: Exploring Muncie's African American Community* (Walnut Creek, CA: AltaMira Press, 2004). For some more recent reflections on the project, in which we discuss in more detail some of the points discussed here, see Elizabeth Campbell and Luke Eric Lassiter, "From Collaborative Ethnography to Collaborative Pedagogy: Reflections on the Other Side of Middletown Project and Community-University Research Partnerships," *Anthropology & Education Quarterly* 41, no. 4 (2010): 370–385; Luke Eric Lassiter and Elizabeth Campbell, "What Will We Have Ethnography Do?" *Qualitative Inquiry* 16, no. 9 (2010): 757–767; and Luke Eric Lassiter, "'To Fill in the Missing Piece of the Middletown Puzzle': Lessons from Re-studying Middletown," *Sociological Review* 60 (2012): 421–437.

4. We approached several university and trade presses, but most scoffed at the idea – except for Rosalie Robertson, who was then at AltaMira Press. Robertson immediately became intrigued with the idea and engaged AltaMira Press as collaborative partners throughout the entire process from beginning to end.

5. Unless, of course, one works in a wealthy university that also expends significant resources on faculty and student immersive learning – and the vast majority of faculty and students do not inhabit such academic institutions today. For more on the Virginia B. Ball Center for Creative Inquiry, see Joseph F. Trimmer, "Teaching and Learning Outside and Inside the Box," *Peer Review* 8, no. 2 (2006): 20–22. For more about the project's unique experience within the contemporary academy, see Lassiter, "'To Fill in the Missing Piece of the Middletown Puzzle'."

6. This last VBC requirement is perhaps the most challenging. For example, each student working on any given VBC project in any given semester must receive a full load of academic credit counting toward their majors or general education requirements so as not to hinder their overall academic progress. For more on this, see the Introduction in Lassiter et al., *The Other Side of Middletown*.

7. Several scholars have pointed out that these are precisely the kinds of contemporary research contexts in which field-based social scientists now find themselves working, whether we like it or not – see, for example, Les W. Field and Richard G. Fox, eds., *Anthropology Put to Work* (Oxford: Berg, 2007). Much of this section's description of contemporary field conditions, however, draws heavily on the recent work of George E. Marcus. See, for example, *Ethnography Through Thick and Thin* (Princeton, NJ: Princeton University Press, 1998); "From Rapport under Erasure to Theaters of Complicit Reflexivity," *Qualitative Inquiry* 7, no. 4 (2001): 519–528; "Multi-sited Ethnography: Five or Six Things I Know about it Now," paper presented at the 2004 meeting of the European Association of Social Anthropology, Vienna, 2005; "Collaborative imaginaries," *Taiwan Journal of Anthropology* 5, no. 1 (2007): 1–17; and "The End(s) of Ethnography: Social/ Cultural Anthropology's Signature Form of Producing Knowledge in Transition," *Cultural Anthropology* 23, no. 1 (2008): 1–14. See also James D. Faubion and George E. Marcus, eds., *Fieldwork is Not What it Used to Be: Learning Anthropology's Method in a Time of Transition* (Ithaca: Cornell University Press, 2009).

8. Marcus, "The End(s) of Ethnography," 7–8.

9. See esp. Marcus, "Multi-Sited Ethnography."

10. See esp. Marcus, "Collaborative Imaginaries."

11. See Lassiter and Campbell, "What Will We Have Ethnography Do?"

12. For more on the history of the development of collaborative ethnographic work in Native North America, see Luke Eric Lassiter, *The Chicago Guide to Collaborative Ethnography* (Chicago: University of Chicago Press, 2005), 25–47.

13. See, for example, Luke Eric Lassiter, *The Power of Kiowa Song* (Tucson: University of Arizona Press, 1998).

14. See, for example, Devon Mihesuah, ed., *Natives and Academics: Researching and Writing about American Indians* (Lincoln: University of Nebraska Press, 1998).

15. For more on the particular contours through which we negotiated such differences in the context of race relations in Muncie, see Campbell and Lassiter, "From Collaborative Ethnography to Collaborative Pedagogy." For more on the productive force of difference in collaborative ethnographic work, see Luke Eric Lassiter, "Moving Past Public Anthropology and Doing Collaborative Research," *National Association of Practicing Anthropologists Bulletin 29* (Washington, DC: American Anthropological Association, 2008), 70–86; and "When We Disagree: On Engaging the Force of Difference in Collaborative, Reciprocal, and Participatory Researches," paper presented at the 107th annual meeting of the American Anthropological Association, San Francisco, California (2008), currently posted at http://www.marshall.edu/lassiter/resources/Lassiter_AAA08 _When-We-Disagree.pdf.

16. Because we are still exploring possibilities, and not yet engaging in what most Institutional Review Boards (IRBs) would consider official research, you should be able to have these informal conversations even if you have not yet begun (or finished) the IRB process. But, as we will discuss in the next section, every IRB is profoundly local, so be sure to clear this with your facilitator or instructor, who will have a better understanding of your own institution's IRB.

17. At the risk of relegating an important point to an endnote, we think it is important to serve food at these large group meetings. At especially important junctures – the first group meeting, for example, or those where critical issues need to be discussed and decided, or at celebrations, or at conclusions – we try to arrange a full meal. These meals do not have to be formal or fancy; in fact, we have found that informal potluck dinners can be particularly rewarding. Beyond the connection and conviviality that comes with eating together, we think potlucks also provide interesting early opportunities for participants to say something about who they are, to act with generosity and care toward each other, and to make a kind of public commitment to the project.

Chapter 3

Emergent Design

In 2005, we moved to West Virginia. Shortly after we arrived, one of our graduate students at Marshall University, where we both now work, learned of our interests in community development. She had been involved in community development for several decades, and wanted to involve us more closely in the state's multiple and various (and often invisible) community development oriented activisms. She first invited Beth to participate in a working group of activists and community organizers pulled together for a private foundation's project that meant to explore the role and meaning of contemporary civic engagement and community action. When that project ended, Beth invited the group to continue the discussion at our home. Before long, a small group of activists and community organizers were meeting every six weeks or so, sharing dinner and conversation. Our discussions of civic engagement and community action (which began to include Eric) soon morphed into discussions about just how the activist histories of specific individuals had taken shape and intersected with other lives and activisms in southern West Virginia. Importantly, we had also begun talking about how elaborating these histories might help us better understand, and direct, our work in activism and community development in the present. We were soon allocating each meeting time for one person to recount her or his life history, and to narrate how she or he ended

Doing Ethnography Today: Theories, Methods, Exercises, First Edition. Elizabeth Campbell and Luke Eric Lassiter.
© 2015 Elizabeth Campbell and Luke Eric Lassiter. Published 2015 by John Wiley & Sons, Ltd.

up doing what she or he does in West Virginia (which, in the case of our group, included community development work in the areas of literacy, substance abuse, domestic violence prevention, environmental preservation, and the arts).

We decided, as a group, to record those sessions, and it eventually became apparent that our discussions had the potential to extend far beyond our small group. A few of us then started recording the oral histories of other local activists and community organizers in the area, many of whom had histories as VISTA (Volunteers in Service to America) workers, and had been organizing in the state's southern coal fields since the 1960s; their stories are virtually unknown to many both within and outside of the state. Though our efforts then were still very personal and exploratory, a few of us did consider the idea that perhaps one day the project might become more ethnographic in scope.

At the time, the group focused primarily on entertaining our various interests and curiosities: namely, how could telling our stories to one another inform, shape, or even change our future activisms? As our explorations unfolded, the "activist oral history project" (as the group came to call it) led us into much more involved discussions about our differing ideas and assumptions about, for example, just who an activist is and what constitutes the work of community development. These expressed differences helped to further our personal (and diverse) understandings of activism in West Virginia, but it also led to a fracture of sorts. The original group eventually split (amicably). We agreed that although we had learned much from each other about how we thought and worked through our own activisms, some of us had a deeper commitment to the overall oral history project than others. Not everyone had the time, the energy, or the desire to expand the oral history collection effort into a larger group of activists and community development workers. The meetings at our home thus ended. Within a year or so, the oral history work also waned, and then ceased as each of us became involved in other projects. One day, perhaps, we – the interested members of the group – may return to our West Virginia activist oral history project. If and when we do return to the project, we expect that it will have turned into something else in the interim, and that it will turn into something else again after it restarts.

Many of our ethnographic projects have begun (and ended or been suspended) like this. Some projects have not entirely "looked like" ethnography at first. Some have begun without clear plans for doing and writing ethnography, for example. But in every case, as opportunities and possibilities began to arise – perhaps in the context of already-existing partnerships or projects, as in the Other Side of Middletown project, described in the last chapter – so did plans for developing more intensely collaborative forms of participation, observation, interviews, interpretation, and writing. Other projects have developed in similarly organic and unspecified ways, but have eventually moved, as the activist oral history project did, in a different direction. Although both of us engaged that group's activities as ethnographers (deploying, for example, ethnographic approaches like recording narratives), the project itself ended without ever developing into something we could pose as ethnography. The group's activities never progressed past an interesting experiment in generating collective and personal understandings of local activisms (which, we want to emphasize, was and is a completely acceptable outcome; it just did not go any further). Still other ethnographic projects, like the university-school collaboration study we described in the last chapter, have begun at the outset with very clear questions for research and very clear expectations for ethnographically based results – even though the trajectory of the research changed as we learned more from the project's participants about the specific dynamics of and expectations for collaboration.

The experience we describe here is by no means unique. All of the above projects, while different in their means and ends, shared a process where inquiry, research, and imagined outcomes developed over time in open-ended, unexpected directions: a fieldwork process of *emergent design* that makes its way into every ethnographically oriented partnership regardless of its initial intent, planned form, or supposed end-product. Emergent design – a view of research that necessitates both creative and practical response to changes in research design as projects evolve – is a particularly important concept to consider when doing ethnography. Given contemporary ethnography's multiple and layered collaborative contexts, all ethnographers must be prepared, perhaps more now than ever, to change plans, expectations, and goals for any number of reasons as any given project develops or unfolds: as new information presents itself, as new questions arise, as old questions become less pertinent, as research contexts shift, as people change their minds, as individuals move on or drop out. And because ethnography is, at its base, with and about people, ethnographers must always be prepared to embrace human shifts and complexities head-on rather than trying to reduce, sidestep, or ignore them.

EXERCISE – INTENTIONAL RECIPROCITY

It has long been the convention in ethnography to think about participation in terms of extended periods of sequestered time. Most anthropology and folklore PhD students – as well as students in a range of other disciplines – who choose to do ethnography, for example, still live for at least a year "in the field," usually in places far different and distant from their own. One of the ideas behind that practice was (and still is) that time led to depth, and that ethnographers thus needed an extended period of on-site time in order to produce their characteristically rich and thick cultural descriptions.

Extended occupation can certainly produce very rich experiences and texts. But collaborative approaches, which have the advantage of a different kind of depth, can lead to experiences and texts that are equally (if differently) rich. Getting to that depth may not require anthropology's traditional and uninterrupted year in the field. But it does require cultivating reciprocal relationships, which means that ethnographers must do more than attend events and conduct interviews. Ethnography is certainly possible without removing oneself to far off and exotic places. But, in our view, it is not possible without meaningful participation: ethnography requires that we commit to being with people, remaining in dialogue, and creating genuine connections.

In addition to cultivating relationships, meaningful participation also asks that we make ourselves useful to the people with whom we are working. We are addressing the issue of reciprocity here, where ethnographers and other project participants intentionally construct mutual benefit in the ethnographic enterprise. In some collaborative work, especially when issues of representation bring people together in the first place, the ethnographic text itself is often viewed as enough. That was the case in the Other Side of Middletown project; in fact, that was the *point* of the Other Side of Middletown project. The text (however construed) is also often the primary point in interpretive exhibits, historic preservation projects, and the like. But a text is not always what collaborators need or want, and a collaborative project must, at least in some way, address the needs of all who participate.

In this Exercise, we ask you to conduct a large group discussion. It is imperative that you involve your collaborators in this discussion for two reasons: first, so that you can decide, as a group, how the project can best serve all of those involved; and, second, because this discussion can – like the "kick-off" meeting we described earlier – cultivate stronger group relationships and deepen your commitments to each other and the project.

1. In smaller groups of 3–5 (but feel free to design these groups in whatever way works best), make lists of at least three "products" you would like to see come out of the project. Be specific, and give your reasons. If, for example, your group and collaborators decide that a shared text is your goal, explain why, and describe the kind of text you want to produce – a website? A pamphlet or book? A film, multimedia presentation, or stage performance? A series of neighborhood posters? (New Orleans' Neighborhood Story Project produces great posters that serve participants in very creative ways. See their website at the end of chapter 6 under

"Suggested Websites.") If you decide on a text, you will also need to suggest how authorship will be determined (who gets credit), who the audience will be, how you will publish and disseminate your text, and so on. If your group decides, as many often do, that they would like help with organizational or fundraising issues, be very specific about what those issues are and what you would like to see happen.

2. Come together as a large group and present your ideas to each other. As much as you possibly can, use consensus decision-making to determine which "products" are reasonable, desirable, and attainable for your group.

As collaborative relationships build, discussions about what partners can do to benefit each other continue to provide ways to strengthen the evolving relationship. You will quickly discover that these discussions are also important venues for genuine collaboration; in fact, at this point in your project, you will likely have begun to notice that you are moving from practicing collaboration to collaborative practice.

By the way, more and more often, research participants are directly compensated for their time and expertise; your group might decide that some form of financial compensation is a reasonable reciprocal action or "product." Although more traditionally oriented ethnographers sometimes object to this practice – and for a range of reasons – we view such compensation in collaborative work – which, again, has much different aims, ends, and applications than other kinds of work – as reasonable and legitimate.

Uncertainty and the Collaborative Process

Emergent design, of course, introduces – or better, acknowledges – additional levels of uncertainty in ethnographic research. But that uncertainty abounds with promise and, especially, collaborative possibilities. As ethnographer and educator Laurie Thorp suggests, embracing this "uncertainty ultimately turns to our advantage; it frees us from the intellectual myopia of hyperdetermined research projects."[1] Understood in this way, ethnography does not emerge out of strictly modeled approaches; it emerges within the evolving, and often tumultuous, processes of human relationships, intellectual struggle, and shared experience.

In her book, *The Pull of the Earth: Participatory Ethnography in the School Garden*, Thorp describes how she learned to "let go" and embrace the ambiguities and uncertainties of doing research on how an elementary school garden might inspire community and change. She reports that as she began the project, she had a difficult time convincing teachers to embrace the goals of her study; she also struggled with deploying predetermined research questions within the context of semi-structured interviews. But as she learned to better appreciate the lived experience of the teachers – by *being* with the teachers on a daily basis – she also realized that much about her original research goals did not fit within the teachers' realms of experience; the research was falling flat. "Time to let go and listen," she writes.[2] And she began to pay closer attention to the stories of teachers and students. To take those relationships more seriously, she redesigned the study in more collaborative terms, so that it "would share the responsibility for research design and surfacing the most pressing questions and issues."[3]

Following emergent design as Thorp did does not mean – in any way – that acknowledging and making room for emergence in ethnographic research leads to work that is haphazard or random. On the contrary: understanding and incorporating emergence opens ethnographers to nuance and complexity; it allows us to be much more adaptable to the changing and unfolding experiential contexts of what we seek to understand. "This uncertainty, this ambiguity of design," continues Thorp, is "indispensable in understanding the lived experience of others. For in our receptivity to the emergent nature of phenomena, we acknowledge a participatory cosmology. Our research design becomes more nimble, adaptable, and exquisitely finessed to the local context of the study and the unfolding complexity of the universe."[4]

Although they may not always call it "emergent design," many other ethnographers have described the process of their research unfolding in unanticipated or unexpected directions in ways similar to Thorp. An example that comes to mind is the work of one of our Marshall University colleagues, Linda Spatig, a professor of education. Much of Spatig's research has focused on evaluation and action research in Appalachian contexts, research often deployed to evaluate, and in many cases, help improve programs or services. One of her many research projects is of interest here, a project with West Virginia activists that ended up unfolding in very different ways than did our own project with the activists described above. In the late 1990s, Spatig began evaluation research of the Lincoln County Girls' Resiliency Program (GRP), a community-based youth development program based in one of the poorest counties in West Virginia. GRP initially sought out Spatig to help them help young women "identify strengths, become active decision makers, and advocate for social change" in their communities.[5] The GRP thrived into the early 2000s, receiving national and regional recognition and funding for a variety of programs from creative song, poetry, and oral history projects to youth-based community development initiatives. But within a decade, these programs began to decline as monies dried up and as the organization and its members faced wave after wave of challenges. During a time of great uncertainty, Spatig and her research collaborators decided to explore together the reasons behind the GRP's decline. The result was their collaboratively written ethnography *Thinking Outside the Girl Box: Teaming up with Resilient Youth in Appalachia.* Spatig describes the decision to shift their previously conducted evaluation research into collaborative ethnography in this way:

> In Spring 2006, I went to Lincoln County and met with Ric MacDowell and Nona Conley, the only remaining board members of the Appalachian Women's Leadership Project (AWLP) – the umbrella organization for the Girls' and Boys' Resiliency Programs – to explore the idea of doing additional collaborative research that would culminate in a book about the youth development work (what ultimately became this book). Over lunch, they sadly confided what I had feared, that the programs were in danger of dying and might not be good candidates for the project. After more discussion with them, and later with Shelley, we decided to move forward with the study anyway – mainly because we wanted to understand what happened. How did programs with such a strong beginning end up in such a vulnerable position? Would the programs survive, and if so, in what form?[6]

The book project would eventually include the board members mentioned above, GRP staff, graduate students, and importantly, many of the youth participants themselves (whom Spatig involved as co-researchers and writers in the ethnography). Although the team's work together turned out to be deeply challenging, at times, even painful (participants describe in several places the heartbreaking experience of watching the GRP program die), in the end, the book is a powerful collective statement about what is possible when people decide to work together for change – even when they do not entirely succeed. It would have been very easy for those involved in the GRP to decide not to write a collaborative ethnography about a program that did not end well. But because the group decided otherwise – and in the process, addressed important questions about the efficacy of community-based youth programs – the book ends up providing powerful evidence for what can happen when we embrace a creative and collaborative process that remains open to the uncertainty, nuance, and complexity of emergently designed ethnography.

Ethics and Ethical Commitments

One critical area in which emergent design factors into any ethnographic partnership is ethics. Many ethnographers work within academic disciplines or professional organizations that have recognized and established codes of ethics, agreed upon principles that detail the rights and responsibilities of those engaged in various kinds of research. In general terms these professional codes share many things, such as doing no harm to others (as in deception or theft, for example), acquiring informed consent from the participants involved in research projects, and representing the aims of research accurately and honestly.[7] Knowing and working within these various codes of ethics, of course, is essential to doing ethnographic work today. But so, too, is realizing that different field partnerships often call for (and call up) very particular sets of ethical commitments between and among those who are working together in a collaborative effort.

One example is the very particular ethical commitment that emerged between Hurley Goodall and ourselves in the Other Side of Middletown project: that we would publish our work for broad dissemination. This commitment was certainly personal. But it was also contextual and historical, representing a particular moment during which we came into contact with one another and planned our collaborative research, as well as the particular – and specifically local – history that made our commitment so critical. As the project unfolded among a much larger group of participants and took the particular form that it did, the discussion around that first commitment developed into ever larger discussions among students, faculty, and community members about what we expected from one another and from the project. These discussions, in turn, became the basis for establishing our own "statement of ethics," an agreed upon set of ethical commitments that students, faculty, and community partners codified as a list of seven explicitly expressed expectations and responsibilities specific to our project. Aside from a statement to "fulfill our commitment to finish … *The Other Side of Middletown*," our collaboratively produced ethical commitments – which included things like establishing transparency in the research process, maintaining openness and honesty throughout, and producing faithful representations – reflected general principles found in most professional codes of ethics. But the commitments themselves as well as the processes we undertook to negotiate and establish those commitments, called up very specific meanings and implications for the members of our group as we dialogued about and developed the book.[8]

Such context-specific negotiations of commitment are common in ethnographic practice, although creating specific ethics statements for particular research projects may be less so. Other examples of these context-specific ethical commitments include issues of confidentiality and anonymity. Several professional codes of ethics acknowledge the rights of individuals participating in various kinds of research to remain anonymous when necessary (such as in an ethnography on, say, illegal activities). But these same codes of ethics also acknowledge – and in some cases, foreground – the rights of research participants to be recognized for their contributions to ethnographic and other kinds of qualitative research. The Oral History Association's "Principles and Best Practices for Oral History," for instance, states in part that "interviewees hold the copyright to their interviews until and unless they transfer those rights to an individual or institution" and that "because of the importance of context and identity in shaping the content of an oral history narrative, it is the practice in oral history for narrators to be identified by name. There may be some exceptional circumstances when anonymity is appropriate, and this should be negotiated in advance with the narrator as part of the informed consent process."[9] The American Folklore Society's (ASF) "Position Statement on Research with Human Subjects," offers a similar statement: "Folklorists guard the confidentiality of their consultants when such confidentiality is requested. In most instances, however, consultants want their contributions to research to be made known. They want to be acknowledged for their contributions and be recognized as community artists and experts in local traditions."[10]

Throughout our own research careers, most of the people with whom we have worked have wanted their contributions to be acknowledged and recognized. That was certainly the case in Eric's Kiowa research mentioned in earlier chapters: in the Kiowa community, song knowledge can be considered a commodity owned by individuals and families (at times literally bought and sold between people), so referencing consultants' contributions was absolutely critical to doing and writing ethnography in that context. Although the Other Side of Middletown's collaborators did not own historical or cultural information in precisely the same way, they still wanted their participation in the project to be respected; they wanted to be acknowledged and cited just as we would reference any other source of information. Still, in both the Other Side of Middletown and Kiowa projects, there were cases in which a few individuals wanted some of their contributions to remain anonymous, especially when they were relaying controversial information that they thought was important to include in the developing ethnographies. As in most ethnographic projects, choosing recognition or anonymity had to be negotiated for each individual case.[11]

Such context-specific negotiations, however, can be much more complicated than just selecting recognition or anonymity. The American Anthropological Association's "Code of Ethics," which is similar to the AFS statement, expresses this point succinctly: "Anthropological researchers working with living human communities must obtain the voluntary and informed consent of research participants.... Minimally, informed consent includes sharing with potential participants the research goals, methods, funding sources or sponsors, expected outcomes, anticipated impacts of the research, and the rights and responsibilities of research participants. It must also include establishing expectations regarding anonymity and credit. Researchers must present to research participants the possible impacts of participation, and make clear that despite their best efforts, confidentiality may be compromised or outcomes may differ from those anticipated."[12] What this often means in practice, it seems to us, is that openness and dialogue about such issues can lead to complicated discussions about just what anonymity or recognition means within its specific context, which can change over time as a project evolves, results are disseminated to different audiences, and various publics respond.

EXERCISE – DEVELOPING PROJECT
CODES OF ETHICS

The regulatory – and very often biomedically structured – ethical codes expressed in many Institutional Review Boards (IRB) are not the only (or, often, the best) guides to ethical ethnographic research. In fact, investigating different disciplinary ethical codes is a useful and illuminating exercise, especially when those codes are compared with IRB codes and applications. Comparing the ethical codes of different organizations in the same discipline is also quite interesting, as is comparing the ethical codes of a single discipline across different national boundaries (say, for example, between the American Sociological Association and the British Sociological Association). Taken together, these comparisons can reveal much about how researchers in particular fields – or allied with particular movements – are expected to both construct and conduct research.

In collaborative projects, researchers must go beyond codified ethical statements and engage ethical practice on much more personal – and interpersonal – levels. Just as research questions can evolve out of the recursive and dialogic processes of early collaboration, project codes of ethics can also emerge out of our evolving project relationships, goals, and commitments.

As we learn more about what we and our collaborators seek to do together, there will come a time when we are ready to "get it down on paper," when we are ready, as a group, to turn our conversations about what we value, what we want to do, and how we want to do it into more formal declarations of our commitments to each other and to our shared project. We have found that collaboratively developing a project code of ethics marks a crucial turning point in an ethnographic project. The process of drafting these codes together does not just document our emerging collaboration, our shared commitment: it is part of the process that strengthens it.

1. Find the full text of three different research codes of ethics (you can use the three offered below under "Suggested Websites," or seek out different ones – say, for example, the Canadian Sociological Association, the Alaska Science Commission, and the American Educational Research Association). Break into pairs or small groups, then discuss the key similarities and differences between the codes. Attend first to visual design: what does each code actually look like? How is each arranged on the page? What are the more distinctive design elements? Then move on to issues

of content. How does each code deal with issues like anonymity and/or confidentiality? What does each code say about to whom knowledge belongs? To what extent does each code either empower or restrict the authority of the researcher and of the researched? Decide which elements of each code you find most relevant to your own project. Still in your small group, write brief summaries of those elements, describing what each says and why you find it relevant.

2. Come together as a large group and discuss. To what extent do different projects, groups, and disciplines emphasize different ethical elements? Why do you think that is so?

3. Create your project's code of ethics. In a large meeting with your collaborating partners, bring and distribute copies of two or three codes of ethics you find particularly relevant to your own project. Discuss each element, and decide, as a group, which you are going to include into your project code and how you want each of them to be written.

4. Using a board, paper, a computer and projector, or some other means of writing and sharing the code as it develops, write out each element in draft form.

5. Once you have finished the draft, go back and, *as a group*, revise the code into its final form. Depending on the size of the group and the nature of the project, having all members of the group publicly "sign" the code can be an important symbolic exercise. It can both strengthen people's project roles and deepen their commitments to each other.

6. Once your Code of Ethics is finalized, make copies and distribute it to all.

Recognition or Anonymity?

The university-school collaboration study we described earlier in the last chapter provides a good example of how ideas about anonymity or recognition can change over time. When we started the project, the research sponsors assumed that research participants would need to be kept anonymous throughout: its participants, it was suggested, needed to feel free to speak their minds about the larger university-community collaborations and not fear reprisal should they relay anything controversial. Simple enough. But the study's "subjects" constituted a relatively small group of administrators, outreach professors, and schoolteachers – much smaller than some of the other projects we have done. Because of the group's small size, and because most of the participants occupied somewhat unique and thus identifiable roles and perspectives, the idea that we could uncritically adopt anonymity, or even confidentiality, across the board was neither reasonable nor realistic. Outspoken outreach professors and schoolteachers, for example, were already known as participants in the overall university-school collaborations, as were the issues about which each cared deeply and the kinds of things each regularly said about those issues. Although we might write our reports with every intention of protecting confidentiality, especially when controversial statements were made, it would be significantly more difficult – and in many cases, impossible – to prevent readers familiar with the project and its participants from connecting the dots and identifying a particular administrator, outreach professor, or schoolteacher. Attempting to guarantee either anonymity or confidentiality could potentially engender a false sense of security and lead some to make remarks that, despite any assurance we might want to make, we simply could not protect from attribution. Better to shift this decision-making to the research process itself – which we did – where research participants, recognized or anonymous, could make explicit decisions about the inclusion of their words in our reports (for instance, participants reviewed – and in a very few cases, struck text from – their interview transcripts before we submitted them for use in public reports).

Some might argue that our consultants may have been much more careful about what they relayed in the context of this particular ethnographic study, and that the research may have subsequently suffered as a result. Both of these possibilities may well have been present, but we concluded that the discussions that emerged from this particular decision-making process actually strengthened the partnership on which the study was founded and, in the end, deepened our understandings of how collaboration worked among and between participants. In any case, because ethnographers deal with people (who have both human and legal rights), such ethical commitments – contextual and emergent as they are – must transcend researchers' "right to know." Remember that ethics and principles of research are always much more complex in the unfolding contexts and emergent design of ethnographic research than they may, at first, seem.

EXERCISE – ETHICS, IRBS, AND OTHER SUBJECTS

Because ethnography involves working with people (in institutional terms, "research on human subjects") contemporary ethnographers who are attached to institutions (universities, primary and secondary schools, hospitals, governments and NGOs, research organizations, and so on) will, in all likelihood, have to apply to some version of an Institutional Review Board for the Protection of Human Subjects (IRB) for permission to conduct their proposed projects. Not all IRBs share exactly the same name – they may, alternatively, be called Independent Ethics Commissions, Research Ethics Boards, Human Research Ethics Committees, and so on – but all do emerge out of the same history and share the same stated goal of establishing guidelines for ethical research that involves human beings.[13]

Depending on the structure, nature, and goals of your own projects, you may or may not have to take them through IRB review. (That is a matter your facilitator or instructor will be better able to address.) If you do have to take your project through IRB, do not let the process intimidate you. Take advantage of whatever formalized training procedures your institution offers, because it will be important for you to learn as much as you can as quickly as you can about how your IRB operates. Although all IRBs are assumed to operate within the same guidelines and principles, the truth is that each IRB is an intensely local affair, animated by people – and institutions – who have particular disciplinary histories and research orientations, varying levels of interdisciplinary experience, and different methodological, curricular, and philosophical perspectives. (Bear in mind that IRBs also differ from each other in terms of time and process; some have designed very efficient, streamlined review processes, while others are notoriously slow.) Although IRBs emerged to redress very real and problematic – and, in some cases, horrifying – research practices, their tendency to pose research in terms of medicine and positivistic science can pose translation problems for those whose research is oriented more toward humanism, collaboration, and action. One of the particular challenges IRBs often present to collaborative researchers – and here we are referring to collaborations with participants in the field rather than with other professional researchers – has to do with, as social researchers Norman Denzin and Michael Giardina observe, the persistent tendency among IRBs to apply "a concept of research and science that privileges the biomedical model and not the model of trust, negotiation, and respect that must be established in ethnographic or historical inquiry, where research is not *on* but rather *with* other human beings."[14] Even though collaborative research approaches can present particular challenges to IRBs that are unfamiliar with them, it is important not to let a lack of experience or understanding on the part of your IRB – with regard to formulaic notions of anonymity or informed consent or community participation, for example – redirect or otherwise undermine your project. Working with IRBs and other institutionally situated ethics committees can actually provide additional opportunities for collaborative practice: the same collaborative elements of dialogue, respect, and shared commitment that build knowledge and understanding in the field can also build knowledge and understanding within your institution.

1. Take whatever IRB training your institution requires.
2. If your project qualifies for Institutional Review, download, read, and study the forms you will be required to submit. We recommend a conversation within your smaller research group (instructors, classmates, fellow researchers, and so on) at this point, so that those who have experience working through the IRB process at your institution can share their knowledge and insights with you.
3. Begin working through your own IRB application, taking every opportunity to share it with your fellow researchers and collaborators as you go. Pay particularly close attention to issues of consent, and what your IRB requires for issues of recognition and anonymity in ethnographic research (see the section "Recognition or Anonymity," discussed earlier). This process will be central to the development of any Consent Forms required for your project (see, for example, the sample release forms available in the "Suggested Websites" section below).
4. As you work, stay in contact with people who work in your IRB office or serve on the IRB committee. Conduct at least one informal interview of someone who serves (or has served) on that committee or works in your research office. If your institutional review board does not have significant experience with collaborative projects, offer examples of such projects that have been successful in other places and ask how best to design the application so that it will address your own site's expectations.
5. Continue working through your IRB application, and asking questions of your more experienced colleagues.
6. Interview institutional colleagues who have successfully navigated your particular IRB. What was the process like? What kinds of concerns did the committee express? What went well? Where were the sticking points? What indications do you have that your IRB is open (or not open) to more collaboratively oriented ethnographic work. If your project depends on the authentic voices of actual agents, how will you write these pieces up?
7. Submit your IRB application, and follow the process through whatever additional requests your committee asks of you.
8. Once your project has been exempted or approved, use this experience to collaboratively write a brief "how to" guide for designing an ethnographic project and submitting it to your local IRB. Compare your guide with others, or with your institution's description of the process, then discuss the similarities and differences.
9. Do what you said you would do in your application, and keep good records. Audits are on the rise, and you could be asked to produce those records.

Issues of Authority: Ethnographer as Facilitator, Research Participant as Counterpart

Thinking about and preparing to do ethnography within frameworks of evolving ethical commitments brings us back to dealing with the complexities of collaboration – as well as its consequences. Among the artifacts of contemporary fieldwork dynamics is a process through which older forms of ethnographic authority situated in the ethnographer have given way to more dynamic, reciprocal forms of knowledge production that are located somewhere between ethnographers and participating groups. Understood in this way, the validity of any given ethnographic project resides not in the presumed objectivity or accuracy of the researcher, but with the project's shared, intersubjective, and emergent research processes. The contemporary ethnographer must set aside any notion of being the authoritative "expert." Other forms of research may encourage or actively cultivate such a stance, but in its intersubjective reliance on others, contemporary ethnography has to be a more humble and honest affair.

Ethnographers have for some time recognized that doing ethnography requires close attention to the politics and poetics of human relations, and that the full range of people who participate in collaborative ethnographic partnerships – not just the ethnographer – bring a diversity of experience and expertise to the table. Though ethnographers may possess deep and extensive knowledge of ethnographic theory and method, as well as other kinds and forms of knowledge, when doing ethnography this knowledge intersects with other kinds and forms of knowledge that are equally deep and extensive. Because these knowledge intersections and interactions have such great potential to complement each other during the research process, respect for others, for others' expertise, and for the collaborative process itself is likely to characterize today's more dynamic ethnographies. The role of the ethnographer, then, is often much more like facilitator; the role of research participant often much more like counterpart, and both of those roles are likely to become even less defined as projects evolve and change.[15]

Once again, it has not always been like this. There was a time in ethnographic research when clear divisions separated the researcher from the so-called subject. In that era, ethnographers collected information by observing and interviewing "informants," whose contributions were something akin to raw material. Ethnographers then sifted, ordered, interpreted, and wrote up the results of that fieldwork in authoritative monographs about the culture of such and such tribe, community, or place. But the former divisions between "the researcher" and "the researched" are much less clear today. In the case of the Other Side of Middletown project, for instance, was Hurley a researcher or a subject? It really is not possible to say. He was both, of course, although sometimes he was more one than the other.

We should point out that Hurley's transient positioning here was – and is – by no means unique, and that everyone involved in the project – including ourselves – inhabited a range of shifting roles, positions, and identities.

The same could be said about the two ethnographies mentioned above, *The Pull of the Earth* and *Thinking Outside the Girl Box*. In both ethnographies, the ethnographers and their collaborators not only share in the research process, they also share much of the space in the ethnographic text itself. Significantly, in both cases, young people (elementary school children in the former, teens and young adults in the latter) are engaged as writing partners, who contribute text and offer diverse experiential perspectives. A chapter written entirely by fourth-grade students in *The Pull of the Earth* makes for a dramatic, but effective, shift in perspective; and numerous youth contributions of poetry, life history, and cultural critique in *Thinking Outside the Girl Box* (which were also collaboratively reviewed and analyzed by the youth researchers/authors) help to craft an incredibly rich portrayal of young women struggling to make a difference in their communities. All good ethnography has arguably done just this, revealing the diverse experience of others. But these contemporary ethnographies are different in how they share authority: while Thorp and Spatig provide the narrative frame through which readers navigate their respective subject areas, their roles are more as "guide" and "facilitator" rather than as the "all-knowing expert." Clearly, ethnographies like these illustrate that the current conditions of the field make what once looked like clear divisions between ethnographer and "subjects" difficult even to see, let alone to delineate.

Such changes in ethnographic fieldwork powerfully call into question, too, the language of traditional ethnographic terminologies like "subject" or "informant," which once helped to reify the divisions between a presumably objective researcher and his or her informing subjects. Many scholars – feminist scholars, for example – have long called into question the use of these terms and the epistemology that gives rise to such notions; so their continued use in ethnographic work seems terrifically outdated, even obsolete, given the current conditions of doing ethnography today.[16] Other terms such as "consultant" and "participant" are problematic as well, but they do seem to be better alternatives, especially as they struggle, albeit imperfectly, within a new language for ethnography that now openly grapples with apprehending the roles and meanings of "ethnographer as facilitator" and "participant as counterpart." We want to emphasize that this is not an exercise in semiotic hair splitting. On the contrary, it raises an important material point: as anthropologist and ethicist Carolyn Fluehr-Lobban suggests, "if a central goal of collaborative research is to work *for* as well as *with* research communities and to develop reciprocal relationships that allow projects to be initiated, discussed, reviewed, and evaluated through a process of continuous consultation and collaboration, *then* the language of the research relationship needs to evolve and change."[17]

So with this in mind, we think it especially important to eschew the separation of self (researcher) from other (researched), and embrace the idea that collaborative ethnographic research is rooted in relationships. Preparing and planning to do ethnography today therefore requires close attention to these relationships, and to the language and meanings that emerge out of the relationships we build in this ever-changing field.

EXERCISE – REVISITING PROJECT LIMITS AND POSSIBILITIES

Throughout the Exercises thus far, we have asked that you regularly and intentionally incorporate dialogue and reflection into the early planning processes – like identifying projects and partners, crafting research questions and goals, and navigating IRBs and ethical codes – because they are integral to the kinds of collaboratively oriented projects we have in mind. These practices are key to what we have elsewhere called being "generous and faithful" in our ethnographic work.[18] Generosity, as we mean it here, is both like and beyond reciprocity: it asks participants to approach each other from positions of openness, compassion, and respect. Faithfulness is a kind of "being true," of operating within the project's agreed upon ethical codes and shared commitments.[19]

The commitments we make to being generous and faithful also carry over into the observation and participation components of our project where, we believe, they may be even more important. Collaborative work depends on trusting and reciprocal relationships: if your aim is to work collaboratively, who you are in the field – and how you are with others – will contribute significantly to your success.

Ethnographers used to talk a lot about "establishing rapport," a process of identifying and engaging key informants, establishing trust, becoming accepted, and so on, with the end goal of "getting inside" in order to gain the "native point of view." These concepts have since been thoroughly complicated and critiqued.[20] But they have not gone away; like other foundational narratives, they have a way of reverberating in the present.

In contemporary collaborations "getting inside" is no longer enough, and "getting the native point of view" is no longer the point. (It is helpful, sometimes, to critically attend to talk like this; words and phrases like "getting inside" and "the native point of view" are rooted in epistemological assumptions that can tell us a lot about how we imagine our work, ourselves, and others.)

We have already discussed, in some detail, the importance of intentionally bringing one's own unique perspective and experience to bear on ethnographic processes, a process that assumes an awareness and understanding of one's standpoint or position when conducting research.[21] Foregrounding issues of position remind us that, of course, it is not possible to operate from a neutral position; everyone has, quite literally, a "point of view." What can be "observed" depends upon who and where one is. (And here we are referring as much to one's personal, cultural, ideological, material (and so on) characteristics as we are to one's physical location.) Moreover, research across disciplines – from psychology to physics – has shown that the very act of observing (or the expectation of being observed, or both) changes what is being observed.

Before you begin thinking about the constructs and processes of observation, participation, and observant participation, we suggest a kind of positionality re-check, a large group discussion that revisits the very first Exercise's discussions (i.e., from the Introduction) about limits and possibilities. Having now identified the people or groups with whom you will work, it is time to think about and discuss how your own subjectivities and positions might express themselves in the project you are taking up. (Although we understand this may not always be possible or appropriate, extending this conversation to the entire group will make the Exercise most interesting and productive.) Here are some questions around which you might organize your discussion:

1. In terms of personal experiences, prejudices, and ideologies, what do you need to be conscious of?
2. In terms of what you are willing to consider or do, or not willing to consider or do, what do you need to be explicit about?
3. Try to describe the group of community collaborators' positions, your class group's position, and your different individual positions.
4. How might (or do) all of those different positions interact?

Suggested Readings

Norman K. Denzin, and Michael D. Giardina, eds. 2007. *Ethical Futures in Qualitative Research*. Walnut Creek, CA: Left Coast Press. A collection of essays that explores ethical issues in ethnographic and related qualitative research. The book includes several helpful articles about navigating ethical issues in contemporary research contexts, including Institutional Review Boards.

Hesse-Biber, Sharlene Nagy, and Patricia Leavy, eds. 2008. *Handbook of Emergent Methods.* New York: The Guildford Press. Examines emergent design and method in a variety of research contexts, including ethnography.

Spatig, Linda, and Layne Amerikaner. 2013. *Thinking Outside the Girl Box: Teaming up with Resilient Youth in Appalachia.* Athens: Ohio University Press. A collaborative ethnography that originally began as an evaluation research project. The work involves research participants in multiple stages of the research and writing processes, and documents the amazing successes, and then the unsettling demise, of the Lincoln County Girls' Resiliency Program, a community-based youth development program.

Suggested Websites

Professional Codes of Ethics and Best Practices – Examples:
   American Anthropological Association – http://www.aaanet.org/profdev/ethics/
   American Folklore Society – http://www.afsnet.org/?page=Ethics
   Oral History Association – http://www.oralhistory.org/about/principles-and-practices/

Cultural Documentation Guidelines – http://www.loc.gov/folklife/edresources/ed-training documents.html A set of guidelines for conducting local field research provided by the American Folklife Center. The site features advice on planning and carrying out fieldwork, including concerning ethics and intellectual property. Of particular note per the discussion of consent forms in the exercise, "Ethics, IRBs, and Other Subjects," see the three sample release forms posted at http://www.loc.gov/folklife/edresources/edcenter _files/samplereleaseforms.pdf

Notes

1. Laurie Thorp, *The Pull of the Earth: Participatory Ethnography in the School Garden* (Lanham, MD: AltaMira Press, 2006), 120.
2. Thorp, *The Pull of the Earth*, 119.
3. Thorp, *The Pull of the Earth*, 119.
4. Thorp, *The Pull of the Earth*, 121.
5. Linda Spatig and Layne Amerikaner, *Thinking Outside the Girl Box: Teaming up with Resilient Youth in Appalachia* (Athens: Ohio University Press, 2013), 1.
6. Spatig and Amerikaner, *Thinking Outside the Girl Box*, 170.
7. See Clifford G. Christens, "Ethics and Politics in Qualitative Research," in *The Sage Handbook of Qualitative Research*, edited by Norman K. Denzin and Yvonna S. Lincoln (London: Sage, 2011), 61–80.
8. For more on this, see Lassiter et al., *The Other Side of Middletown*, 20–21.
9. Oral History Association, "Principles and Best Practices for Oral History," http:// www.oralhistory.org/do-oral-history/principles-and-practices/ (accessed March 10, 2014).

10. American Folklore Society, "AFS Position Statement on Research with Human Subjects," http://www.afsnet.org/?page=HumanSubjects (accessed March 10, 2014).

11. For more on the ethical negotiations that emerged within these two contexts, see Luke Eric Lassiter, *The Chicago Guide to Collaborative Ethnography* (Chicago: University of Chicago Press, 2005), 85–97.

12. American Anthropological Association, "Statement on Ethics: Principles of Professional Responsibility," http://www.aaanet.org/profdev/ethics/upload/Statement-on-Ethics-Principles-of-Professional-Responsibility.pdf (accessed March 10, 2014).

13. For the purpose of simplicity here, we use the term IRB throughout to refer to the range of institutional ethics boards and committees concerned with these and similar regulatory functions.

14. Norman K. Denzin and Michael D. Giardina, eds., *Ethical Futures in Qualitative Research: Decolonizing the Politics of Knowledge* (Walnut Creek, CA: Left Coast Press, 2007), 25 (emphasis in original).

15. See George E. Marcus, "The End(s) of Ethnography: Social/Cultural Anthropology's Signature Form of Producing Knowledge in Transition," *Cultural Anthropology* 23, no. 1 (2008). See also Paul Rabinow and George E. Marcus, with James D. Faubion and Tobias Rees, *Designs for an Anthropology of the Contemporary* (Durham: Duke University Press, 2008).

16. See Carolyn Fluehr-Lobban, *Ethics and Anthropology: Ideas and Practice* (Lanham, MD: AltaMira Press, 2013), 165ff. See also, for example, Lila Abu-Lughod, "Can There Be a Feminist Ethnography?" *Women and Performance: A Journal of Feminist Theory* 5: 7–27; Deborah A. Gordon, "Worlds of Consequence: Feminist Ethnography as Social Action," *Critique of Anthropology* 13, no. 4 (1993): 429–443; Ann Oakley, "Interviewing Women: A Contradiction in Terms," in *Doing Feminist Research*, edited by Helen Roberts (London: Routledge & Kegan Paul, 1981), 30–61.

17. Carolyn Fluehr-Lobban, "Collaborative Anthropology as Twenty-first-Century Anthropology Ethical Anthropology," *Collaborative Anthropologies* 1 (2008): 175–182 (emphasis in original).

18. Where noted, parts of the following discussion are excerpted from and/or build upon sections from Elizabeth Campbell, "Being and Writing with Others: On the Possibilities of an Ethnographic Composition Pedagogy," PhD diss., Indiana University of Pennsylvania, 2011.

19. Excerpted in part from Campbell, "Being and Writing with Others," 187.

20. See, for example, Les W. Field and Richard G. Fox, eds., *Anthropology Put to Work* (Oxford: Berg, 2007).

21. See, for example, Sandra Harding, "Rethinking Standpoint Epistemology: What is 'Strong Objectivity,'" in *Feminist Epistemologies*, edited by Linda Alcoff and Elizabeth Potter (New York: Routledge, 1992), 127–140.

Chapter 4

Engagement: Participant Observation and Observant Participation

In the summer of 2002, Traditional Arts Indiana (a partnership between Indiana University and the Indiana Arts Commission), together with the Indiana Historical Society, launched a project (funded by the National Endowment of the Humanities) to document Indiana's county fairs. The project grew out of an urgent sense that the state's farms and fairs were in the midst of accelerating change, and that traditions long associated with the state's agricultural past were in flux: "Indiana is in a critical period in its cultural and economic history," Traditional Arts Indiana (TAI) noted at the time. "As more and more Hoosiers leave the farm, local economies rely less on agriculture, and the rural cultural landscape becomes more diverse. Historically rooted in the effort to strengthen agriculture by educating farmers and their families, county fairs have been important community gathering places of celebration and ritual, offering a wealth of opportunities to document a segment of life in Indiana during a time of change."[1]

Three teams, each made up of one folklorist and one photographer, were sent out to document these socio-cultural and economic changes, each team to a different county fair. Beth and photographer Rich Remsburg constituted one of these folklorist/photographer teams; they were assigned to the state's largest county fair, the 11-day Lake County Fair in Crown Point, Indiana. The two arrived in Crown

Doing Ethnography Today: Theories, Methods, Exercises, First Edition. Elizabeth Campbell and Luke Eric Lassiter.
© 2015 Elizabeth Campbell and Luke Eric Lassiter. Published 2015 by John Wiley & Sons, Ltd.

Point on the afternoon before the Fair's opening day, then spent the evening wandering the fairgrounds, searching out previously arranged contacts, introducing themselves to strangers, and striking up conversations. That night, Rich also took some photographs; Beth began arranging interviews and scribbling fieldnotes. Both then spent the full run of the fair – each of the 11 days, from opening to closing – doing some version of these same things.

If Rich's photographs covered the broad range of what he saw at the fair, Beth's fieldnotes covered the broad range of what she experienced there, from equipment malfunctions to emotional connections to intellectual revelations. At the end of each wickedly hot August day, Beth worked from the brief notes and jottings she had taken throughout the day to produce expanded fieldnotes. The pages excerpted in what follows began as bare scribblings as she walked the fair each day, were rewritten as expanded fieldnotes each night, and were further expanded and polished (for publication on the TAI website) when she returned home at the end of the fair's run.

Although events more clearly related to the ethnographer's experience than to the site under study are not always highlighted in public fieldnotes, we have chosen to include excerpts from Beth's fieldnotes because we think they illuminate the value of heightened attention in the field, and demonstrate that our notes serve sometimes to document what we see, sometimes to record what we think, and sometimes to craft understandings.

The first of these fieldnote excerpts begins with an account of Beth's attempt to solve a sudden and serious technology problem: on Day 7, her (expensive) professional Marantz audio recorder had stopped working, so she had run out in search of a cheap replacement.[2] Unfortunately, it looked like that was not going to work so well either:

(Day 8 Fieldnotes): Called Eric last night about the CD recorder. He hesitated, then suggested that this was probably not the best route for me. This is not an ideal situation for learning a new technology, especially not for someone as technologically impatient as me.

So I'm standing at the entrance to Best Buy at 8:50am this morning. It opens at 9:00, and I am not the first person there. As I wait, more people walk up, and by 8:58 or so, there must be 15 people waiting to get in. Meanwhile, inside, the crew is doing some kind of nutso happy getting ready for the day pep rally. God, I'm glad that I don't work for a chain. They let us in at a few minutes past nine, and I exchange the CD recorder for a plain old tape recorder. I'm going to take the Marantz to that electronics shop, but I've got little faith that they can fix it, and I don't want to have to come back over this strip mall hell avenue. So I buy the recorder now, assuming that I'll need it later.

But the Marantz is restored!! … It turns out that it was both the cord and the input jack on the actual machine. In the back of my head I'm thinking that carrying the machine around like a pocketbook (clunk, bang, clunk, bang) for 10–15 hours a day for the last 8 days … might have had something to do with this. It takes a few hours, but by 1:00 this afternoon, I'm back in business.

I head over to the midway to talk with one of the game operators. Rich met and struck up a conversation with her and introduced me to her yesterday, and I'm glad to have met her. I've found that most of the folks on the midway don't want to talk very much, so I'm delighted that he's found someone who will. She is a hoot. She was born and raised right near here. When she was a junior, she got a summer job with a carnival outfit at this very Fair. The following year, after she graduated, she left town with the carnival. That was a long time ago. She's got some interesting insights about people, she's a real student of human behavior. We'd earlier talked about some of her insights, not on tape, and I'm hoping that she'll talk more about that.

Suddenly, her whole demeanor changes. Her voice drops, her eyes drop, and she says, "I got to get back to work now." Her boss has spotted us. This is not good. I'm struck by her change, I ask if I've gotten her into trouble, and she says that she can talk to whoever the fuck she wants to talk to. But she's not talking to me anymore, that's for sure. I ask her to point out her boss and she does. About twenty yards away from us is the Boss, a hard looking woman in shorts, a yellow T-shirt, visor and sunglasses. Looking at us, not smiling. I need to do something so that she does not catch it for this … I approach the Boss, all big smiles and sorority friendly. Boss is cold, suspicious, does not return grin … Boss says I need to go by the office, that they'll hook me up with someone who will take me around. I can't just go up and start talking to people. Not allowed.… The secretary, who sits in the office trailer behind a thick glass window is just as cold as the Boss. She'll call someone to take me around, and after ten or fifteen minutes, a large man comes by. Big, dark glasses, and cold like the rest. But eventually we get comfortable. These folks are not cold, not really, they're just terrifically suspicious. Mostly because they're constantly getting screwed by local media or police or both. I've got a microphone and I'm wandering around talking to people, so I must be doing the next big "Carnies are scumbags and lowlifes," piece. One of the other operators expressed some of this as well, when we talked to him the other day. It's not just about what people think of carnies either, says the big guy, it's that what they think has real consequences. They're constantly hassled by law enforcement. And every year somebody or a few somebodies get hauled off for things they haven't done. If anything happens and the carnival is in town, we're always the first suspects. I wonder if they're as innocent as he says, but truthfully, this is the first time I've ever heard the "carnie" response to how they're publicly perceived, so I set it aside and listen. He introduces me to another game operator who tells a story that's chilling. One of her summer employees … was taking pictures for a scrapbook. Spent too much time (according to the police) taking photos of kids jumping on the moon walk, so he was arrested, and his camera and laptop were seized. They didn't find anything, but they charged him with felony disorderly conduct. So now he's got a felony on his record. And this kind of stuff happens all the time. So they have to be very careful.

She got started in this business in 1980 by working a game. Now she owns games of her own, she has become an independent contractor. Like everyone else, she lives in Florida during the off season. Not a bad life, really. She works 8 months and has four months off. And there is a real chance to get ahead, if you're smart, you play by the rules, and you save what you can. She enjoys the work. Earlier, Rich had observed that a lot of these game operators tell or show people exactly how to play successfully, but that people don't pay attention. On this rope game, for instance, and I ask her about it, they'll tell players exactly how to do it, then demonstrate, and people still do the wrong thing. She laughs again. She's quick to laugh. People don't pay attention. You can tell them, step by step, and they won't listen. We tell them how to do it, for example, right hand, left foot, move fast, keep low and don't think about it. But they go up high, hand, hand, foot, foot. And then when they do finally figure it out, when they've heard us say it enough times and they've got the right idea, they think about it too much.

My last interview with the carnival folks is with one of the managers. This is an eye opener. In fifteen minutes, he completely redefines the carnival. This is no quaint, historic, and slightly dark cultural expression. It's a business. A growing business. An aggressive business with a strong business model ... his driving vision, idea, concept is that the proliferation of competition for your entertainment dollars (resorts, casinos, Six Flags, Disney) means that if we want to compete we have to professionalize. Come up with standards. Enforce those standards. Uniforms, shaded resting areas. And we'll come up with a rating system that will grade amusement companies based on how they comply with these standards, like the Michelin guide. A two star company might be uniforms and clean staff. Three star might be that plus a certain number of cooling stations. Four star might have shaded resting areas in addition to what's required of two and three star ratings. Standards. He is on fire. He's intense, he's leaning forward, he's a businessman consumed. He talks about how pacesetting companies in California set new standards for the egg industry. His industry is on the crux of a change. Smaller companies cannot bear the cost of insurance, and of million dollar rides. And they don't have the resources to comply with all of the many regulations that hit this business, from trucking regulations, to food safety, to the drug and alcohol testing that his company and others now do regularly. We're sitting in the drug testing trailer right now. And he doesn't just provide drug tests, he provides housing (bunk trailers), commissaries, transportation to doctors and Laundromats. It's all too much for the small mom and pop companies. And large companies are the wave of the future.

The carnival employees are changing as well. He looks for college students, sharp, clean-cut kids with whom the public can be comfortable. He regularly brings in workers from other countries, again, young, sharp people without that "carnie" edge.

He doesn't say this exactly, but I think that this is what he's saying, that is, about the "carnie" edge. I pick it up in the way that he emphasizes the new kinds of employees he's bringing on. College students, pre-med and pre-law. He's moving away from the old carnival, elevating this to the status of legitimate business.

It takes me awhile to recover, and I wander around the midway, looking at the employees and envisioning the way all this will look in twenty years. Clean cut college boy employees will still be here. But an old time carnie's observations about human nature might not be. I think, too, about the fascination with the carnie image, about how we've romanticized this life, in a dark and dirty way, granted, but it's still romanticized. Well, it's in the process of being sterilized now. In a generation this will be a radically different place.[3]

Beth's daily fieldnotes were a critically important part of the documentary project not just because they helped her keep track of what she was experiencing, but because the experience of writing, referring back to, and revising those notes regularly led her to important insights. Her stance in the notes is also deeply personal and particular; rather than presume an objective stance, all of the project's photographers and folklorists were encouraged from the outset to bring their unique perspectives and experiences to bear on the process. Her unique perspective – personal, subjective, positioned – is clearly evident in these notes; but much like photographs – which are, of course, also personal, subjective and positioned – her notes represent a snapshot, a fleeting intersection of time, place, persons, and events viewed through a very specific and particular lens of experience. Had Eric – or you, or anyone else – been there instead, the notes would have been very different.

We will return to Beth's notes from Day 8 of the Fair several times throughout this chapter, and use the notes as we consider problems and issues associated with participant observation, take up the art of observant participation, and briefly explore the various and multiple ways encounter and experience are both eschewed and embraced in the practice of writing fieldnotes.

EXERCISE – ONE SCENE, MANY POSITIONS

Doing ethnography today often blends reflection and action, and reminds us to stay aware of how our own positions (e.g., our own backgrounds, perspectives, ethnocentrisms, likes and dislikes) might manifest and influence our ethnographic work. In one of our favorite pedagogical exercises, we ask a group of students (and, depending on their desired degree of participation, project collaborators) to document the same scene from different angles, or at different times, or to simultaneously document different sensory aspects of the same scene, and then to compare notes. We have also found it very rewarding to do this Exercise twice in a row. On the second time through, we ask students to shuffle their groups and positions, and to "observe" with different people and from a different point of view.

In the last several decades, it has become commonplace for contemporary ethnographers – and contemporary ethnographies – to reflexively position themselves – personally, theoretically, historically, experientially, and politically – within the ethnographic scene.[4] That means that many ethnographers often eschew authoritative positions of "objectivity" and instead seek to be more honest and open about the lens (experiential, theoretical, political, etc.) through which participation and observation transpire. In addition to the honest grounding reflexive positioning makes possible, we believe that it also has tremendous constitutive potential. For that reason, we see value in reaching beyond the practice of introducing oneself (or one's group) at a narrative's outset or situating oneself at various points within the ethnographic narrative. When reflexive establishments of position are made public and shared processes, they become ways for project participants to meaningfully introduce themselves to each other, and to begin identifying places where their different interests, motivations, and passions might overlap. Introducing and maintaining these processes can cultivate those overlaps, thereby strengthening the project's shared commitments and enhancing the overall collaboration.[5] With this in mind, try the following:

1. Write solo accounts or descriptions of a single scene or happening. (This is an exercise you can also do with photographs, films, material objects, websites, and a host of other cultural artifacts.) Be sure to incorporate all of your senses, and to make notes of your impressions, questions, and reflections as you write.
2. Trade your notes with a partner, then discuss what each of you wrote. Based on what you already know about yourselves (and, if relevant, about each other), why do you think you saw what you saw or missed what you missed?
3. With the same partner, write paired observations of another event (or artifact). Feel free to discuss your observations as you write. When you are finished, trade your notes and discuss what each of you wrote. In addition to the questions above, talk with each other about how the

experience of writing simultaneously was different. How did it affect what you saw and wrote?

4. Engage your large group in a discussion about this practice of observant participation. What kinds of things do most of you observe? What do most of you miss? If you could go back to either scene or happening, what would you pay more attention to? How was the experience of shared observation different from the experience of solo observation? Think here not just about *what you observed,* but about *how you and your partner observed together.*

Participation

When TAI hired Beth to document her impressions, observations, conversations, and reflections via daily fieldnotes, they understood that the process itself – of immersion in a particular setting – would provide a specific kind of field-based knowledge that surveys or brief interviews or focus groups alone could not achieve; a documentary record that would, in the present and in the future, offer an intimate, up close and personal, "on the ground" view of county fairs. This vision of knowledge-generation represents a particular way of framing direct, lived experience: that the ongoing and unfolding intersections of individual experiential histories generate particular and intersubjective ways of knowing unique to human encounter, which thus provide unique opportunities for understanding.[6] This way of thinking about the links between experience and knowledge was similarly reflected in Eric's work with Kiowas in southwestern Oklahoma (briefly noted in earlier chapters). As his first ethnographic project on Kiowa song unfolded in the early 1990s, many Kiowas insisted that although dialoging about song traditions was absolutely critical to song knowledge, it was not enough: Eric needed to learn more about singing Kiowa songs by *singing* Kiowa songs with Kiowa singers at various community events. Only continual engagement with singers and singing, many suggested, would prompt the deeper forms of knowledge and understanding that Eric sought in his broader ethnographic work on song.[7]

Doing and writing ethnography itself rests on an analogous idea, that direct participation and genuine engagement in the day-to-day lives of others can provide unique insights into how various and diverse ideas and activities generate meaning. Many ethnographers thus take the seemingly simple idea of participation in the lives and activities of others very seriously – even given differing formulations of "the fields" in which we work today (as discussed earlier, in the chapter on "Fields of Collaboration"). Ethnomusicologists Timothy Cooley and Gregory Barz, for example, write that "the old fieldwork with all of its assumptions and expectations is dead. Yet, the epistemological efficacy of experience has lost none of its luster. The face-to-face interaction with individuals and some level of participation in the music-cultural practices we hope to understand … [still] lends itself to meaningful musical 'being-in-the-world' today.…"[8] Although they are writing about ethnomusicology and the dialogic process of "being in the world" through shared musical experience, the changes in fieldwork to which Cooley and Barz refer here also apply more generally to all kinds of ethnographic work.

As we have noted in earlier chapters, until relatively recently the assumptions and expectations behind ethnographic participation – especially in disciplines like anthropology, folklore, and ethnomusicology – usually involved long-term fieldwork (a year or more) in a place far away from the comforts of home (usually abroad, and usually in non-white, non-Western settings). These assumptions and expectations find their roots within emerging forms of ethnography in the late nineteenth and early twentieth centuries, but the Polish-born British anthropologist Bronislaw Malinowski is most often credited with designing a systematic method for doing fieldwork that put direct participation in the service of day-to-day ethnographic observation. In his 1922 *Argonauts of the Western Pacific* – perhaps his most well-known work – Malinowski argued that documenting the "*imponderabilia of actual life*" must be "collected through minute, detailed observations, in the form of some sort of ethnographic diary" via close, long-term and ongoing participation. This meant living in the village or community, learning the language, participating in daily life, and conversing with "the natives," all the while collecting, as Malinowski put it, "ethnographic statements, characteristic narratives, typical utterances, items of folk-lore and magical formulae … given as a *corpus inscriptionum*, as documents of native mentality."[9] Malinowski thus maintained that this way of doing (we might say "inhabiting") fieldwork brought ethnography a step closer to achieving, as he famously wrote, "the final goal, of which an Ethnographer should never lose sight. This goal is, briefly, to grasp the native's point of view, his relation to life, to realise *his* vision of *his* world."[10]

Before Malinowski's time, much of what passed for ethnography (although certainly not all) involved knowledge collection from so-called informants via thematic or topical interviews, often collected during periodic trips to a particular locale. Though there were many notable exceptions, back then ethnographers did not usually take up residence "among the natives," as it were. Malinowski, it is sometimes said, moved fieldwork "off the verandah" (verandah being a metaphor for older styles of fieldwork where ethnographers interviewed informants on the covered porches of the homes of colonial administrators and missionaries) and into the villages and communities where people lived their daily lives. Malinowski's insistence on systematic, direct, daily, and long-term participation and observation helped to usher in a new era for ethnography, one characterized by what would come to be known as "participant observation."

The American school of anthropology, particularly under Franz Boas at Columbia University, also pushed ethnography in this direction, as did several ethnographers in the field of sociology, such as W. E. B. Du Bois, Beatrice Potter Webb, and Robert and Helen Merrell Lynd.[11] Most notably, the deployment of urban ethnography by the sociology department at the University of Chicago (often called the Chicago School) employed systematic, direct, long-term participation and observation among urban groups ranging from gangs to policemen, who were studied in ways comparable to how Malinowski and other anthropologists studied tribal groups.[12] By mid-century, participant observation fieldwork was firmly ensconced in the ethnographic tradition. From then on, any budding ethnographer – whether planning to study a mountain village, an urban factory, or two towns' schools – could expect to spend a year or more in the field, working in the vein of what is now often called the "Malinowskian tradition" of ethnographic fieldwork.[13]

In many ways, the so-called Malinowskian fieldwork tradition is still very much alive. Many academic programs (especially in anthropology, where ethnography remains a mainstay, but also in fields like folklore, education, sociology, and so on) still expect doctoral students, in particular, to spend extended periods in the field as a kind of "rite of passage" for doing ethnography.[14] Eric's doctoral research (with Kiowas), for instance, followed this trajectory. Such extended field experience, whether conducted abroad or at home, continues to be valued. (Many urban ethnographers, for example, point out that touch-and-go surveys miss the deeper complexities of serious urban problems, and that sustained fieldwork has much to offer in this regard.)[15] And as in Malinowski's time, ethnographic participation still implies a very *particular* kind of engagement in the lives of others: it is more than just "play" or "performance" (which "participation" might imply on the surface). As Beth's fieldnotes illustrate, this kind of participation takes careful notice of others' ideas and activities as well as one's own, and pays special attention to when and where differing conceptions and experiences come across one another. (Often, insights arise at those intersections.)

Given this shared intellectual and experiential history, though, ethnographers think about and conceptualize fieldwork in radically different ways today. Few if any ethnographers would assume, for example, that they could study "isolated" or otherwise "bounded" cultural groups in ways Malinowski or the members of the Chicago School once did. And the world continues to shrink, of course: people and things travel more easily and at much greater speeds (ethnographers may, for example, come and go to and from multiple field sites); we live and work in worlds that now blend the virtual and the material (ethnographers may, for example, participate in groups sitting at computers in their homes or offices); and, importantly, an increasing number of ethnographers now work within and study communities, organizations, or groups to which they already belong.

In addition to the more collaborative contexts in which ethnographers now work, for the past several decades such changes in fieldwork have forced serious reconsiderations of the traditional assumptions and expectations behind participant observation. Make no mistake: ideas of participation – which imply engaged immersion – and observation – which imply active documentation – continue to be the hallmark of ethnographic work. But the tension between the two – where participation implies a close, intimate connection with others and observation implies a distanced separation from these same others – has motivated a reformulation of participant observation. We take up this issue in the next section. But before we do, we will return to the next part of Beth's Day 8 fieldnotes:

I wander back to the midway and head for the top end, near the racing pigs and Rick West's trailers. I look for him, but he's not with the 12 foot alligator, nor is he with the world's biggest pig or smallest horse. I ask the woman at the horse booth if she knows where Rick is. She's not sure, but if I'll mind the stand, she'll go look for him.

I sit in what is now my booth. Rick's recorded voice surrounds me. "A cupful of water and a handful of grain is all it takes to feed the little Wizard. A tiny little horse, with feet the size of silver dollars. A horse smaller than a bale of hay. He's alive, he's real." Behind me, in his pen, the little Wizard looks up, his head cocked, curious, immediately aware of my foreign presence. He knows he does not know me, but he doesn't seem alarmed. Just curious. A sharp black eye stares up through a fringe of mane. I laugh. Don't worry, little Wizard. It's only temporary. On the desk in front of me is a simple cash box, filled with quarters and a few one dollar bills. To my right is a pencil, and a few pieces of paper. Nothing else. I look up, out, and over the midway. At the game booths, at the exhibit buildings, at the huge rides in the distance. I'm surrounded by noise. Rick's bally; the jointy across the way who's calling people in to play her "water chasin', water racin', havin' fun with the water gun" game; the guy at the next game down who's telling players how to toss rings over bottlenecks. Patriotic songs on the loudspeakers. People walking by, some of whom look up at me and my little horse. The little Wizard. "Come on up," I yell. "He's cute!"

I'm alive. I'm real. Four kids come stomping up the short steps to see the little Wizard, and I take their quarters. They want to know if they can pet him. I tell them no, he'll bite. It seems like the appropriate response. Wizard is now interested in the kids. I get the sense that he's used to snacks from strangers. I am so into this.

Rick is walking toward the trailer, walking fast, an odd look on his face, but almost laughing. "She put you to work!" He's almost incredulous. I'm suddenly self-conscious. I feel like I've been busted, but only for a second. It was fun, I say, and I got you four. I give the regular back her post, and we walk in search of a shady spot. He's still teasing me about the recorder. It's fixed, I say, and he says it's a good thing because it makes me look legit. I've been thinking the same thing all week. As we walk, he talks about modern day freak shows, about Jim Rose's Circus Side Show, an act that's out there today, and all of Rose's crazy antics, from walking on broken glass to strange piercings. Rose does college shows, and the content is slightly different that it may have been years ago, but this extreme stuff today appeals to the same side of us that freak shows did years ago.

From an early age, Rick West was fascinated by the freak shows.[16] He remembers fairs and carnivals from his childhood, the preserved two-headed baby he wasn't allowed to see and the live two headed cow he did see. He bombarded the cow's owner with questions, about how he fed and cared for it, what it did, etc, and says that from then on he was hooked. He began in this business by helping out his uncle, who had acquired a 3100 pound steer and was taking it around to fairs and carnivals in the upper Midwest. Rick was showing that steer when he heard about a two headed cow in Saskatchewan. He bought that cow and showed it for almost two years. It had a reaction to penicillin given for pneumonia and died. That was a real shame. But he's been at this ever since. He imported some huge, poisonous, and insane lizards from Thailand in the late 1960s. He went to pick them up at the airport, and the customs people were very suspicious of a guy with a ponytail picking up boxes from Thailand, so they wanted to open the boxes. He warned them against it, but they insisted. They changed their minds after the lizards started thrashing and thumping around in the boxes. He carried around a huge horse for a while too, a 2800 pound horse named Big Jim. He brought Big Jim to this very fair, and people from here still remember him, still ask about him. The miniature horse, Wizard, has been with him for 14 years.

These shows have changed a lot over the years. It's become bad form to show "freaks," whether human or animal. We had talked about this the other day. It's no longer appropriate (or legal?) to, for example, set up "life shows," sets of fetuses, each individually preserved in a bottle (they used to be called "pickled punks"), and arranged chronologically, from least to most developed. But in the industrial building, the anti-abortion people have a fish tank filled with water and floating fetuses. They're not real, but they're so incredibly life like that they could be. You could never set that up on the midway, but in another context, – hey, it's ok.

I'd actually been thinking about Rick's analysis this morning, as I waited in the electronics (and appliance) store for my recorder to be repaired. A dozen televisions played, and several featured the Sally Jessie Raphael show. Sally had a man and his son as her guests this morning. The boy, perhaps about four, had an extremely rare birth defect, which left him with an extreme case of hydrocephalus, and a range of other unusual features. The pretext was this: Sally (and the boy's father) hoped that by bringing the boy on national television, by showing him and talking about his symptoms, that some doctor somewhere with some experience and knowledge, might know about this ailment and about possible treatments. But, it seemed to me (especially after my conversations with Rick), that Sally was having herself a "freak show."

Did she have the boy on display in the hopes of a cure? Or in the hopes that gawkers would lead her show to higher ratings? And either way, who was benefiting? Not the father or the boy, who surely weren't paid a ton of money to go on the show. The show benefited, of course, because people would certainly stick to a sight like this. So now the "freak show" has become disguised, and someone other than the "freak" profits. Interesting.

Rick concurred absolutely. They know what they're doing. They're appealing to that same piece of us that can't help but look at a car accident. We can't take our eyes off the "abnormal." It's human nature. In the old days, he says, it was more honest. I ask if he thinks people would still go to freak shows today. He laughs again. Absolutely. If he set one up on that midway right now, people would line up to see it.

Things are changing. I reflect on my earlier visit with the carnival manager and Rick talks about how expensive it is to actually set up on the midway anymore. They used to practically give the space away. But it's valuable real estate now, and those million dollar rides are slowly pushing everything else off the midway. They're easier, in a way. You only have to pay and take care of one guy with those rides. A lot less complicated than the platoons they used to travel with.

Rick thinks his days are numbered. In five or ten years, even the mild shows like his will be gone. Animal rights activists will see to it, he says, even though he takes much better care of his animals than most do. Imagine what life that hog would have had. A few miserable months on a factory farm floor, confined to a pen barely bigger than himself, then off to slaughter. Or, if he was lucky, a few years as a stud boar, still in a cage, and then off to slaughter. This hog has the life. He gets regular food and water, and he's got a fan and cooling spray down there to keep him from overheating. They stop, regularly, on the road, to check up on the hog and cool him off. And then in the off season, he's got his very own pasture, right next to Wizard's as a matter of fact, where they spends their days laying around, sleeping, and trading stories of the road.

Back on the midway, I think about the way things are changing. I'm cheered by the terrifically turn of the century sound that the Carousel's music has. I tell the operator so, and he agrees that it's great. He gets it right off the Internet.

INTERLUDE: EQUIPMENT CHECK

Fieldwork is much more complicated than it seems, and that includes the processes of organizing and preparing for it. In addition to issues of epistemology, philosophy, and ethics, fieldwork is also rife with practical, logistical, and technological challenges. Think about the fieldnotes that began this

(Continued)

chapter: Beth's (hitherto reliable) professional recorder malfunctioned on Day 7 of the Lake County Fair, and if she had not been able to (quickly) find an old-fashioned radio repair shop the overall project might have been seriously compromised. It has been our experience that these kinds of events happen with some frequency. Equipment inevitably malfunctions. Even when the equipment works well, sometimes the operator does not. It may be hard to imagine yourself doing this, but at some point in nearly everyone's ethnographic career someone has forgotten to turn the recorder on. Or has left her notebook at home (with the consent forms). Or has not brought power cords, or SD cards, or batteries ... you see our point.

If we had been writing this book 10 years ago, we would have written a detailed discussion about specific kinds and brands of field equipment, especially field recorders. In this period of rapid technological change, however, such a discussion would become almost instantly obsolete (though we do offer some very basic advice below). Still, ethnography requires field equipment; even without discussing the pros and cons of particular kinds of recorders, there is still plenty to talk about.

When you are choosing your recorder, think about how you intend to use your video and/or sound files. If you eventually hope to broadcast your files, you will need very high-quality recordings. Regardless of your broadcast medium – whether podcast, website, film, or radio – you will need rich, clean recordings that are free from noise, distortion, and the host of other glitches to which contemporary recordings are prone. For the best quality sound, use a high-quality external microphone. At the risk of making statements that are blindingly obvious, make sure that the recording devices you use are compatible with your computer equipment, and organize your equipment well ahead of time. (That last trick has been especially helpful for Beth because organization does not come naturally to her.) Keeping all of this in mind, consider the following:

1. In general terms, first decide what quality sound or video you want to capture and make sure your equipment can capture it. As much as possible, use an external microphone. And make sure your recording equipment is compatible with your computer equipment.
2. We think that, at the very least, every ethnographer should have a high-quality audio recorder. Fortunately, the expense of such recorders is no longer as prohibitive as it once was, and digital formats have opened up a wider range of possibilities. When choosing a recorder, we recommend the following:
   a. Choose a (digital) recorder that includes a computer interface (via USB, for example) that allows you to easily transfer recorded files from the machine to your computer.

b. Avoid at all costs recorders with proprietary recording formats. Only choose a recorder with widely available recording formats (MP3 or WAV, for example), formats that can be used across multiple programs and platforms (PCs and Macs, for example) without the use of software designed for the recorder only.

c. Recorders that include a jack for an external microphone are, we think, essential for fieldwork. With an external microphone attached to the recorder, you will have the option to place the microphone at some distance from the recorder itself. In addition to better sound quality, you will also be able to move, start, stop, or pause the recorder without those actions becoming part of the recording itself. (Without an external microphone, for example, simply moving the recorder across a table can cause an enormous amount of unwanted noise on the recording.)

d. Digital recorders with the above options can be found at many local office stores (Staples or OfficeMax, for example) for a reasonable price. But if you are interested in investing in a high-quality digital field recorder (audio or video), several electronics stores carry these (such as B&H Photo Video in New York City). We often use "The Sound Professionals" (see www.soundprofessionals.com), which carry a highly diverse selection of high-quality recording equipment. (More information about digital audio recording equipment is referenced below in the "Suggested Websites" section.)

3. Designate a particular case that will hold all of your equipment, ideally one that is divided into discrete sections. A briefcase might work, or a small rolling suitcase, or a backpack or messenger bag. Decide where in the case you will put your recording equipment and cords; writing utensils and notebooks; laptop, netbook, or tablet; back-up supplies, and so on. Then (and this is important), get in the habit of putting things back in their places.

4. Always have the bag packed, ready to go, and in a readily accessible place; that way, when it is time to use it, a quick check through to make sure everything is present and working is all you will need to do (rather than a frantic search for all of your different bits and pieces).

5. Test all of your batteries, carry extras, and always make sure your power cords are in the bag.

6. As a final part of this exercise, make a list of your equipment needs and all the possible issues that might arise with each piece of equipment. Discuss this list with your instructor/facilitator and/or classmates.

From Participant Observation to
Observant Participation

In the fieldnotes that open this chapter, it may have seemed that Beth's inclusion of the Marantz recorder's repair had little to do with her fieldwork. It certainly seemed that way as that August morning gave way to the day's events and activities. But as she describes in the fieldnote section immediately above, her brief encounter with the televised Sally Jessie Raphael show in the electronics store and repair shop turned out to prompt an important insight later in the day – about "freak shows" in this case – that, in turn, prompted further dialogue with Rick about the changes transpiring at county fairs. Experience can be like this, of course: seemingly unrelated encounters can often turn out to be pivotal, especially as we move to couch various and diverse experiences as story. And so can doing ethnographic fieldwork, which requires much more of us than just watching and recording sights, sounds, tastes, and feelings as they occur: ethnographic fieldwork demands that we open ourselves to the process of observing experience itself, reflecting on that observed experience in the moment, and seeking out dialogue with others as this reflexive practice unfolds.

This way of thinking about and representing participation and observation, which places experience at the center of ethnographic documentation itself, is sometimes called observant participation. Building on, but reformulating participant observation, this process very explicitly foregrounds how one's own experience shapes one's interpretation of others; builds on the processes of subjectivity and intersubjectivity; and focuses attention on those points where "co-understandings" between and among people surface. In the midst of much discussion about the problems elicited by participant observation in the 1980s and 1990s – when ethnographers across the social and human sciences continued to question how the presumed science of ethnographic work had considerably narrowed the full potentials of the craft – anthropologist Barbara Tedlock put it this way:

> Recently there has been a subtle yet profound shift in ethnographic methodology, from the oxymoronic concept of "participant observation" toward the observation of participation. During participant observation, ethnographers move back and forth between being emotionally engaged participants and coolly dispassionate observers of the lives of others. This strange procedure is not only emotionally upsetting but morally suspect in that ethnographers carefully establish intimate human relationships and then depersonalize them – all, ironically, in the name of the social or human sciences. In the observation of participation, on the other hand, ethnographers use their everyday social skills in simultaneously experiencing and observing their own and others' interactions within various settings. This important change in procedure has resulted in a representational transformation where, instead of a choice between

writing a personal memoir portraying the Self (or else producing a standard ethno-graphic monograph portraying the Other), both Self and Other are presented together within a single multivocal text focused on the character and process of the human encounter.[17]

Tedlock is describing the emergence of narrative ethnography, a kind of ethno-graphic writing that highlights the storied relationships that give rise to ethno-graphically based co-understandings. Many ethnographers, like Tedlock, recognized that participant observation deployed in the field had helped to create clear divi-sions between self and other – that is, between ethnographers and the people with whom we work – often established in fieldwork practice and then reified in the texts ethnographers subsequently created. Ethnographers often wrote their "official" eth-nographic reports in distanced, objective, and scientific frameworks (the "observa-tion" side of the formula); and wrote memoirs of fieldwork in frameworks that underscored participation, immersion, and friendship (the "participation" side of the formula). In her analysis, Tedlock forces a number of important questions: Why not collapse these divisions – or do away with them entirely – through frameworks of observant participation assembled as narrative in a single ethnographic text? Instead of eschewing experience, subjectivity, and story in the name of some sort of presumed "objectivity," why not embrace them? Why not use the full range of experience to our advantage as ethnographers?[18]

For many, this turn toward observant participation helped to resolve, in part, the tensions inherent in participant observation (between the presumed positional differences of "objectivity" and "subjectivity," for example) and provide more honest, realistic ways for doing fieldwork and ethnography. These developments, of course, furthered the idea that ethnography was not a scientific enterprise in search of some sort of "objective" knowledge untethered from human experience, but that it could be better understood, once again, as an intellectual effort in search of *understanding* between and among people.[19] In many ways, though, such a shift made doing and writing ethnography much more complicated: no longer could experience, subjec-tivity, and story be set aside as a kind of observational or perceptual "bias." If experiential processes were to take their place in the larger constellation of ethno-graphic theory and practice, then they would have to be accounted for in all of their complexities. (We will come back to this point shortly.)

Tedlock's emphasis on narrative ethnography implies that observant participa-tion very purposefully constructs ethnographic documentation as story at all levels – in final ethnographic forms as well as in the forms we create in the so-called field, forms like fieldnotes. For those interested in collaborative work, fieldnote forms are particularly important to consider because, above much else, they highlight the processes by which participation, engagement, and experience give rise to the eth-nographic understandings that unfold through the processes of fieldwork. Although a host of different documentary processes are now in use, we continue to believe that fieldnotes – writing what we experience and writing about what we experience in the field – are critical to the development and production of contemporary ethnography.

Fieldnotes: From Definitions, Meanings, and Practices to Storied Observations

To situate just what we mean by all of this – that observant participation really is a reformulation of conventional participant observation, and that fieldnotes, constructed as story, can and should be at the center of this process from the very beginning of ethnographic work – we need to backtrack a bit. Just what are fieldnotes? Why are they so important? And what role do they have to play in the construction of ethnography within contemporary collaborative contexts?

If ethnography rests on the idea that direct participation and genuine engagement in the day-to-day lives of others can provide unique insight into how various and diverse practices and activities engender meaning, then fieldnotes both document and drive the fieldwork processes that struggle to actively make sense of how those meanings are constructed – and *co*-constructed – in everyday experience. Ethnographers Robert Emerson, Rachel Fretz, and Linda Shaw write that "fieldnotes inscribe the sometimes inchoate understandings and insights the fieldworker acquires by intimately immersing herself in another world, by observing in the midst of mundane activities and jarring crises, by directly running up against the contingencies and constraints of the everyday life of another people. Indeed, it is exactly this deep immersion – and the sense of place that such immersion assumes and strengthens – that enables the ethnographer to inscribe the detailed, context-sensitive, and locally informed fieldnotes … [as] 'thick description.'"[20]

But as ethnographers work toward this "thick description" (an idea often attributed to anthropologist Clifford Geertz, who famously wrote about ethnography as thick description), they collect and document a host of different things at different places and at different times.[21] As such, ethnographers differ about the meanings of, as well as what exactly constitutes, the texts we call "fieldnotes." This is especially true today as "the field" does not always imply the kind of clear separation of sites it once did (as in from "home," for example, or from "home culture"). For example, noting the tensions evoked by participant observation, anthropologist Rena Lederman writes that:

> being in the field involves placing oneself deliberately in a context of commitment doubly different from the normal one. As we all know, this act need not involve any traveling at all: it sometimes involves simply a shifting of attention and of sociable

connection within one's own habitual milieus. From this perspective "the field" is not so much a place as it is a particular relation between oneself and others, involving a difficult combination of commitment and disengagement, relationship and separation.[22]

The "fieldnotes" part of the field experience may also not quite be what it used to be, or at least, what it used to seem to be. And although definitions and meanings of "the field" and "fieldnotes" have been and are intimately tied to one another, these definitions and meanings can vary widely among ethnographers.

For some, fieldnotes comprise the daily notes written while in the field – however that "field" is construed – which may or may not include the kind of expanded notes that we feature here in Beth's fieldnotes; such fieldnotes are often distinguished from other kinds of field documentation (such as surveys, photographs, or audio and video recordings). For others, the category of fieldnotes might also include daily logs and journals or diaries or blogs, as well as interview transcripts and the like. For still others, fieldnotes can incorporate a much wider range of fieldnote records associated with a particular project, and might include notes taken while technically not "in the field" (from research in archives, ongoing academic study, or discussions with colleagues (which could include things like letters and emails)).[23]

Though ethnographers may have different ideas about the definitions and meanings of fieldnotes, the fieldwork practice that gives rise to these records can no doubt involve a wide range of different writing activities that occur both in and out of the field.[24] Let's turn back to Beth's fieldnotes for a moment. During the day when she was physically at the Fair, she wrote brief notes about her observations, conversations, and reflections as they occurred (or as soon as possible thereafter) in a narrow reporter's notebook, stuffed in the back of her waistband. Those notes – which we have referred to as *scribbles* or *scribblings* – included things like sights, sounds, tastes, feelings, names, statements, questions to ask, and questions to follow up on, often in the form of mnemonic cues that she could later use to write her expanded fieldnotes after she had left the fair for the day. In most cases, she scribbled very brief notes while conversing with others, and wrote more extensively between conversations, on the way to and from events, or during a break (when eating, for instance). On some days, she found herself with more notes than she could reasonably write out. Those notes were expanded in the field as much as possible, then expanded again and polished (for style, mechanics, and grammar (for the purposes of clarity more than correctness)) after the field component of the project had come to an end.

Using such scratch notes to serve as the basis for writing expanded fieldnotes is common.[25] But as one might expect, ethnographers often go about logging such notes very differently. Eric, for example, prefers using a small hand recording device to make personal spoken notes while "in the field," which he uses at a later time to fill out daily logs and write expanded fieldnotes. Others may rely much more on so-called headnotes – encounters, memories, and other "mental notes" not necessarily written down, but that still serve to document part of a given fieldwork experience.[26] However we choose to make our notes in the field, this very basic and simple fieldwork procedure firmly positions us in the tension between participation and observation, where the "particular relation between oneself and others, involving a difficult combination of commitment and disengagement, relationship and separation" is most immediately, and intimately, experienced.[27]

The processes that engage us in writing fieldnotes can be, at times, very disconcerting for both ethnographers and our interlocutors. Some ethnographers describe field contexts in which taking notes openly in front of others seemed especially uncomfortable or even impolite, particularly when it violated social norms; others describe making scratch notes discreetly so as to avoid highlighting their "outsider" status.[28] In extreme cases, inscribing notes may even invoke suspicion or outright conflict. Eric, for instance, describes one of his first fieldnote-taking experiences thus:

> In a study that I did as an undergraduate on drug addiction and recovery, I attended Narcotics Anonymous meetings to get a sense of the recovery process. At my first meeting, I started taking notes, as any anthropologist might. The meeting came to an abrupt halt and all eyes turned to me; everyone wanted to know what I was doing. Because anonymity is such an important foundation of Narcotics Anonymous, my behavior of taking notes was highly inappropriate. Was I a reporter? A cop?[29]

While this encounter could perhaps have been avoided had a bit of prior attention been paid to the norms and expectations of Narcotics Anonymous (NA) meetings, it nonetheless illustrates how embodied fieldnote practice can underscore the problems of participant observation. As an artifact of the fieldwork process, this experience and its accompanying discordance may be unavoidable. This may be true even when, at the outset of a project, ethnographers endeavor to be absolutely clear and honest about the goals of their work (which is, of course, critical to the ethics of doing ethnography); it may even remain true as time passes, and we and our ethnographic collaborators become acclimated to this odd fieldwork practice. (Eric's NA consultants, for example, soon became accustomed to his note-taking; even still, after that first debacle, he never took notes at meetings again.) Yet as we craft our headnotes and scribbles and scratch notes into expanded fieldnotes (traditionally, sitting alone at our computers at the end of the day) and then into our ethnographies (traditionally, sitting alone at our computers at the end of a project) we find that we *do* have choices as to how we will deal with the experiential tension between self and other (and all that goes with it). Whether, on the one hand, we choose to sidestep or ignore that tension or, on the other hand, centralize or problematize it, is up to us. In making the latter choice, observant participation begins to come back into the picture.

EXERCISE – DEVELOPING YOUR OWN (FIELDNOTES) STYLE

For much of its history, ethnography's primary artifacts have been texts. In fact, many have defined ethnography as an inescapably textual practice; after all, there is a reason it is called ethno-*graphy*. Over the last several decades, calls for ethnography to be less centered on inscription and more oriented toward dialogue, performance, activism, and so on have increased. We heartily agree with the idea of expanding ethnography's possibilities into those and similar arenas. Ethnography does not necessarily have to result in traditional texts, but in our view, constructing texts is as central to ethnographic practice as observant participation and meaningful participation. Moreover, it has been our experience that in collaborative work, both the processes of creating texts and the texts themselves provide still more opportunities to build relationships, negotiate understandings, organize actions, and strengthen the ongoing collaboration.

We devoted a significant amount of time and space to fieldnotes in this book, and to foregrounding the central role of the author (or authors) in those notes. We observed that fieldnotes require us to take careful notice of our own and others' ideas and activities, and to pay special attention to when and where differing conceptions and experiences come across one another. (We also remembered to pay close attention to the ambiguities of "agreement," when perceived agreed-upon goals or values may be masking unchallenged assumptions or beliefs.)[30] We have discussed, at some length, the idea that field experience is deeply subjective and positioned, and that fieldnotes both document and drive the processes of actively trying to make sense of everyday experience. Fieldnotes are also a way to turn that experience into storied description, a fundamentally human way of pushing for connection and toward understanding. One of the reasons we included such extensive excerpts from Beth's fieldnotes is because we believe that fieldnotes, constructed as story, are (and should be) at the center of ethnographic work. It is helpful, we think, to read your notes (and the notes of others, of course) for stories. What kinds of stories do you encounter? Which stories are most powerful? Which are most telling?

Although we have both come to embrace a very storied fieldnotes style, when we were first being trained as ethnographers, we were introduced to many different ideas about and methods for writing fieldnotes. We learned about double-entry notes (which separate observations from interpretations), descriptive notes, jottings, running accounts, sketches, maps, and so on, and about a host of reasons and methods for doing each. We have since also encountered fieldnotes as audio recordings, data tables, short stories, short-hand, and more. Our styles have evolved over time, and now we each write our notes in different ways. Beth started out with double-entry notes, but kept losing track of the differences between sides; now she mostly jots down impressions, phrases, and the outlines of events, sights, and scenes; then she drafts and re-drafts. Eric started out writing out double-entry and descriptive notes, but found it was not fast or spontaneous enough to keep up with his observations and ideas; now, he audio-records ideas and descriptions in the moment, then transcribes and expands them later. Because fieldnote styles are so subjective and particular, we like to ask students (and, when relevant, project participants) to experiment with different fieldnote styles and methods, paying attention to what they find most and least useful about each.

In this Exercise, we ask you begin experimenting with different ways of writing notes "in the field," and that you start conducting regular and explicit conversations with your fellow writers about which styles work or do not work for you, and why those styles work or do not work. Here are some styles you might try (in the context of attending an event, for example); your facilitator or instructor will most certainly have others:

- Freewriting: The goal here is to just keep moving. Identify a set time period and write down everything that comes into your head, without censoring or editing. Do not stop, and try not to get distracted when your thoughts start taking off in different directions. Just keep writing.
- Continuous narratives or descriptions: This is a slightly calmer and more intentional version of the above. The idea here is to capture the full outlines of stories, or to collect as many fully formed sensory details about an event (or person, or place, etc.) as you possibly can.
- Double-entry notes: This tried and true style of fieldnotes records both what is going on (from your position, of course) and what you think (or feel, or wonder about, or how you interpret what) is going on. Generally, you split a page down the middle (or make a two-columned table), and keep your observations on one side, and your interpretations on the

other. (Your instructor or facilitator will have specific recommendations about how to use double-entry notes.)

- Scratch notes: Scratch notes are a kind of "in the moment" way of recording key words or phrases related to important happenings, sights, sounds, impressions, comments, and so on. The idea with scratch notes is to jot down those key words or phrases in the moment, and use them to jog your memory as you construct your fuller account later. (A word to the wise, here: it is best to turn scratch notes into fieldnotes as soon after you take them as possible, before the memories to which they are attached fade completely away.)
- Reflective audio recordings: More and more fieldworkers are using audio recorders to collect and keep fieldnotes. Recorders are tremendously versatile in the field, and they can capture a range of note-taking styles and modes, from scratch notes, to sensory descriptions, to reflections and questions. Provided you have permission, you can also use recorders to capture events. Remember, though, that a recorded event is not a fieldnote. Recordings become fieldnotes only when they interact, in the moment, with fieldworkers' ideas, responses, reflections, questions, interpretations, and so on.
- Annotated images: Digital devices have made it so easy to collect, keep, and annotate images that an entirely new and very visual method of fieldnote-taking is now possible. Just as those who are aurally oriented might find audio recordings helpful, researchers who are drawn to the visual might find particular value in collecting still or moving images – again, provided they either are in an environment where such recordings are allowed or they have explicit permission to collect them. Here too, though, remember that visual materials are not, in and of themselves, fieldnotes.

Whatever style (or styles) you eventually adopt, remember that fieldnotes both record sensory and intellectual perceptions *and* provide opportunities to observe and reflect on the unfolding field experience. Just as comparing what you observe with what others observe can be of great value, comparing your fieldnotes with others' can be an enlightening experience. We have found that comparing or sharing our fieldnotes with others – whether between ourselves or within larger groups – can lead to a host of new insights. Just as different people observe differently, and from different experiences and perspectives, they also write differently, and about different things. We have also found that sharing fieldnotes is an excellent way to make relationships stronger and collaborations deeper. A caveat here: if you intend to share your notes with others, or to make them publicly available, you must write your notes accordingly. We do not advocate that you gloss or censor your notes. But it is important, we think, to point out that the writings you intend to share will always be different from those you keep to yourself. Be vulnerable or critical or offensive in your scratch notes, if that is your bent. But be thoughtful about how you transfer those qualities into your final notes.

On Fieldnote Forms

How we choose to think about, position, frame, enact, and represent our work in the field is very closely tied to the rhetoric of description. Historian James Clifford points out that ethnographers' use of oft-cited metaphors like "thick description" frequently gloss the diverse and various ways that written texts and other forms of documentation actually emerge in and from the field. Clifford observes that field-work involves a range of engagements with inscription (i.e., turning our attention to write down things observed, such as when making scratch notes); transcription (i.e., recording and translating statements made by others, such as in an interview); and description (i.e., forming coherent accounts of some sort of socio-cultural reality, such as in expanded fieldnotes on a county fair or a Narcotics Anonymous meeting). Each of these writing activities produce different kinds of texts, texts which can range from, for example: scribbles, essentially codes or other mnemonic cues for scratch notes; to interview transcripts for interviews; daily field narratives with beginnings, middles, and ends; and to expanded fieldnotes that include inter-pretations and analyses. But no matter what form the fieldnotes take, it is critical to remember that they are never independent from the prism of interpretation; they are never innocent texts. Fieldnotes are always mediated by history, experience, and perspective. In this sense, they are deeply rhetorical constructions that, quite liter-ally, *authorize* very particular ideas, attitudes, and compositions of reality. When we make scratch notes, we make choices about what we attend to and what we write down. When we transcribe others' speech, we make choices about the questions we ask and the meanings we ascribe to responses. And when we write out or otherwise polish our expanded fieldnotes, we make choices about how to frame, analyze, narrate, and interpret encounter and experience.[31]

Our fieldwork choices emerge out of and enact larger imaginaries (again, imag-ined enactments and outcomes) for doing and writing ethnography. Those imag-inaries are, in turn, inextricably linked to larger histories of ethnography. Clifford suggests that as Malinowski and other ethnographers of his time moved fieldwork "off the verandah," fieldnote forms followed suit. As ethnographers sought to further distinguish their ethnographic descriptions from previous forms of ethnography – as well as from colonial and missionary accounts, travel writing and other "non-scientific" forms of cultural description – multiple forms of inscription and transcription gave way to a more singular mode of fieldnote description that both reflected and informed the assumptions surrounding what were then the scientific goals of ethnographic work. While ethnographers like Malinowski encouraged direct participation in the daily lives of others, as well as the need to discern and report the "native point of view," the fieldnote forms (and the ethnographies these kinds of notes shaped) that emerged along with the shift toward science further accentuated the "turning away" from encounter and experience. (This is a particularly persistent and thorny problem: if, for example, inscription (as in scratch notes) momentarily turns us away from social interaction, then fieldnote descriptions – written alone, at the end of the day, and without the input of those with whom we work in the field – take us another step further; studies written up when one has "returned from the field" take us further away still.) Importantly, fieldnote forms associated with the then emerging emphasis on science also diverted attention away from the collection of native texts (life histories, for example), which had been more common in older, historically oriented forms of ethnography; separated out and privileged the idea of "observation" unencumbered by the experiential bias of the observer (a consequence of which was to reformulate ethnographers' perceptions and analyses as "ethnographic facts" or "data"); and which ultimately authorized the ethnographer-cum-expert to speak on behalf of others, a position reified in scientific ethnographic accounts.[32]

As Tedlock observes, the contemporary ethnographic tradition thus inherited clear divisions between (scientific) ethnographic accounts and (humanistic) memoirs, between ethnographers (as experts) and the people with whom they worked (as subjects/informants), and – of course – between participation and observation. Though such divisions were thoroughly interrogated and deconstructed in the 1980s and 1990s, they have proved remarkably persistent. Many field manuals helped to sustain such divisions well into the 1960s and 1970s, regularly recommending, for example, that fieldworkers keep personal views or interpretations out of fieldnotes; some ethnographic texts and practitioners advocate such positions to this very day. In this view, fieldnotes are the province of "objective" data; "personal" ideas and observations belong in a separate field journal or diary.[33] Of course, nothing is inherently wrong with keeping a field diary. We all have a right to the intimate feelings and concerns that inevitably arise in our encounters with others, and we may not want to publish everything we think, experience, and encounter in a public fieldnote entry. But many, if not most, contemporary ethnographers now agree that fieldnotes, in particular, and fieldwork, more generally, can no longer be formulated as innocuous collections of raw, unbiased, or unmediated "data" to be simply translated into detailed, thick description. Ethnographic description is even more than multivariate and multileveled: it is an inherently mediated affair that is always surfacing historically, politically, and rhetorically between and among people.[34]

This does not mean that anything goes for fieldnotes, or that one's prejudices or ethnocentrisms do not matter (they most certainly do). It also does not mean that the very idea of fieldnotes is hopelessly compromised. What this attention to fieldnote constructs and traditions helps us to understand is that writing fieldnotes can and should be a more honest affair where, for example, ethnocentrisms are "on the table" rather than hidden; where one observes self and others through the lenses of both training and experience; and where one's participation is mediated through dialogue and story, instead of viewed through the presumed lens of detached "objectivity." Being an observant participant and writing storied fieldnotes will not do away with the awkward disjunctures and feelings brought on by "turning away" to inscribe, transcribe, or describe. But it will allow us the occasion to deal with these disjunctures and feelings more openly and directly rather than pretending they do not exist.

The position that ethnographic description is ultimately a mediated affair that is always surfacing historically, politically, and rhetorically between and among people also means, of course, that fieldnotes are always written for *someone* or some combination of *someones*. In many of the collaborative contexts in which ethnography is now put to use, fieldnotes are assumed to have a range of audiences: ourselves of course; participants, sponsors, funders, or institutions; disciplines and careers; activist or political aims; and publics both known and not yet known.[35] This position contrasts sharply with more traditional constructs of fieldnotes as raw (and private) materials used to craft the final (and public) ethnographic text. Although, in some cases fieldnotes have eventually been deposited in public archives (and, in some rare cases, have been unexpectedly subpoenaed), many ethnographers still report that they rarely intend for others to see their notes.[36] In collaborative contexts, though, fieldnotes are not accorded any assumed privilege of privacy. The conditions and expectations of collaboration often create circumstances in which fieldnotes – along with other fieldwork materials – are positioned, from the very onset of the project, as open and public records. (Beth's Lake County Fair fieldnotes are an example.) The same has been true in some of our other ethnographic work. During the Other Side of Middletown project, for example, student fieldnotes were publicly available, shared and discussed with community consultants, and eventually placed in a publicly accessible university archive.[37] Though these kinds of approaches to fieldnotes are by no means new or unusual, they are increasingly common in today's collaborative field contexts.

The way these notes are written and framed matter, of course, when additional audiences come into play. And in contemporary collaborative contexts, additional audiences *always* come into play, pushing us to be as honest, direct, and explicit as we can about how participation, engagement, and experience shape the ethnographic understandings that develop and unfold in fieldwork. Such contexts also lead to an appreciation that the processes of fieldwork are, inevitably, more complex when positioned in this way.

EXERCISE – WRITING WITH

In the collaborative work we have done over the last 20 years, and especially in the Other Side of Middletown project, we have become increasingly aware of how writing, and especially writing together, can create understanding and transform relationships between people. That has led us to collaborative writing approaches in which we write *with* rather than *about* others.[38] We write *with* not just to get our stories straight or to "give voice" to *the* other, but as a way of negotiating our understandings of *each* other; writing *with* underlines our connections to, rather than our distances from, the people with whom we work. It becomes a kind of shared scrutiny that makes us aware of our *selves* in the world together, and a practice of shared reflection that carefully and generously makes and explores connections to the people with whom we work and write.[39]

There are many different ways to write *with* others. Students working on a project together, for example, could trade their own fieldnotes back and forth – or share them with community-based project participants – and then use both the notes and the dialogues about those notes to write or co-write the project's texts. Another kind of writing *with* could ask differently positioned collaborators to produce joint texts, or to produce a compiled collection of single-authored texts (with or without grounded reflections). Indeed, there are many possibilities. If you decide to deploy collaborative writing, the particulars of your project and situation should determine the particulars of the writing *with* you choose.

In previous Exercises, we have suggested several combinations of short writing exercises and small- and large-group discussions that (we hope) have helped you to decide what you would like your project to be, as well as what kinds of "texts" you would like your project to produce. Just as you had to investigate your project possibilities at the beginning of your project, you will now have to investigate the writing possibilities that are available to you and your collaborators. This will likely be a challenging process: there will be, at the very least, differences of position, of interest, of expertise, of orientation, and of aims to bridge. Literacies will be different, language traditions will be different, and the amount of time (and desire) people may or may not have will be different. It is important to thoroughly discuss the details of how you will proceed.

As you discuss and decide, however, be aware that like collaboration itself, collaborative writing is a profoundly contextual, and sometimes unwieldy, process. Be prepared to regularly revisit and revise your collaborative writing plans and practice; in our experience, a project's writing processes are among its most fluid. Those who initially agree to write may find they do not have the time or interest; initial plans to have all participants co-write may go awry if radical differences in voices and perspectives emerge.[40] When you encounter these kinds of differences, remember that they are inherent to collaborative practice and that working through them will be difficult, but necessary. Just keep in mind that encountering and working through difference is one of collaboration's key aims.

Gather together those who will be writing together (or those who you think, at this point, will be writing together) and talk through the following questions:

1. Who will do the writing?
   - Will everyone produce actual pieces of text? Or will it work better if all (or some) contribute notes and/or ideas, and others work those contributions into drafts?
2. Who will be responsible for which pieces? Will you write synchronously, in pairs or teams? Or will you write privately, and then meet to review and combine the texts?
   - In your first discussions about this particular issue, emphasize that this will remain an open issue for some time, and that it remains open for discussion. If the first arrangements you make do not work as you hoped they would, come together and make new arrangements.
3. How will you review and/or revise each other's texts?
   - It is very important to remember that a person's writing is her personal expression. Egos are deeply involved in writing, and so it is critical that you establish explicit guidelines for how writing will be reviewed, and how decisions about what writing will be included will be made.
4. What process will you use to decide what goes into the final text, and what does not?
   - You can certainly revisit this issue as the project moves on, but it is best to get this particular discussion started early, and to make decisions

about how this process will work before you have any actual text to evaluate.

As composition, community literacy, and service learning scholars have by now made abundantly clear, there are a host of different ways to write with others. Each of those ways suits different kinds of collaborations, operates differently, pushes toward different ends, and builds different kinds of relationships.[41] Eventually, by remaining open to your project, your collaborators, and the vagaries of writing processes, you will settle on a set of practices that work best for you.

By Way of Conclusion ...

We will return to several of these issues in the next two chapters, but for now, we offer the conclusion of Beth's fieldnotes from that wickedly hot August day:

It's late afternoon, but not yet suppertime. That's probably a good time to catch the guy who runs the Grange Cafeteria. I'm hungry, too. Another good reason to go. There are only 15 or 20 folks eating at the Grange right now, so it is a good time. I go through the line quickly. I get fried chicken, spinach (again), cantaloupe, and cornbread. I see the manager, and call out to him. When can we set up a time to meet? This is as good a time as any, he says. Go sit at the staff table and I'll be right over. I see that the staff table is one of the ones that has a fan. I'm thrilled, as these tables are always hard to get.

The manager is not a typical Grange member, at least not by the old standards. The Grange originated as a rural organization, made up primarily of farmers. He's not a farmer; he's a businessman. He joined 28 years ago at the suggestion of a neighbor. Though he "got off easy" at first, he's since become primarily responsible for this cafeteria at the Fair. It's a huge ordeal. The building is only a pole barn, and it has no real sides, so they can't store anything in it. Every year they take their stoves and refrigerators and freezers and cash registers and tables and everything else out of storage, then bring it up here to set up. It takes a few days. And then a few more to clean it all up since it's been sitting all year. Then there's the food ordering, the hundreds of meat loaves they make ahead of time, finding all the help they'll need to run it each year. It used to be staffed entirely by volunteers, Grange volunteers, but every year the membership dwindles and those who are left get older and older, and now they have to pay people to work here. Still some volunteers, but more and more paid staff. It's the primary fundraiser for the year for the Grange, yet each year it seems like they work a little harder and make a little less. It's that way for a lot of organizations, he says. People don't want to join anymore. They sit at home and watch TV. And each year there's a rumor that this will be the last year, but it's hard to say exactly when that last year will come. As long as I can still do it, he says, we'll keep doing it. At about 60, he is one of the younger members. And it doesn't seem like there's anyone coming along behind him. Still, he enjoys doing this. And it makes him feel helpful, useful. And he does run it very well, so he'll keep going for a while longer yet. I ask him about changes to the Fair over the years he's been here and he laughs. He's not sure he even knows what's out there right now, let alone twenty some odd years ago. He never leaves the cafeteria, never really has. He laughs again. I couldn't tell you what's different. I couldn't tell you what's the same! He scolds – during the time we've been talking I've let my dinner get cold. It's time for me to eat, he says, and for him to get back to work. He gets up, straightens his white T shirt and white apron, and bids me farewell. I tuck in. Damn this spinach is good.

Rich has been taken by the display of convict art that the local sheriff's office has put out, and wants me to go see it. In the very back of the building, behind the DARE sheriff's car and the stern young men in brown uniforms are three stern women behind a row of glass cases. Masks, dice, crosses, made of prison paper maché, toilet paper and water. Aluminum foil scissors, not functional, but a lot of this stuff is. Can be used as a weapon. Lots of weapons. Combs, pens, toothbrushes, carved, sharpened, made into shanks or shivs. Soap, molded and put into a sock becomes a soap jack, a hard weapon. Same with latex paint. They peel the paint and form it into a hard ball, same thing. They can really hurt someone with that. As we go through the cases I'm struck by the creativity, the ingenuity; the Warden, agrees. Yes, they have a lot of creativity. A lot of them are very smart. And if they'd used all their talent positively instead of negatively, they could have really gone somewhere in their lives, benefited society. But instead they bring pain to people and are a burden on society. It's a drag to have to confiscate this stuff, but anything that's used for something other than its intended purpose is contraband. We just can't have it. Maybe they'll make weapons. Anything they make can turn on them. A pretty box made of cards can become desired by some other inmate and provoke a fight. Or be stolen, same thing. These wonderful religious necklaces, they're beautiful, but an inmate can hang himself or someone else with one. And you know, everybody gets religion in prison. And they get upset, why you won't let me keep my cross? But they can't have that. It could be a weapon.

From the sheriff's display I wander into the Pigeon and Rabbit barn, another suggestion of Rich's. Stanley, the superintendent of the pigeon show sits at a table facing the main entrance. Stanley races pigeons, as did his father, who was also superintendent of the pigeon show here. Stan's father had birds when he was young too, birds were all over those European neighborhoods. Polish, Germans, Belgians, English. They all had coops out back, they all did the racing. We talk about feeding and conditioning, about caring for and training the birds, about the business of racing, about his past races. Stanley is very friendly, but also very low key. The highlight of our conversation comes when I ask him what it's like to see his pigeons come home. His face lights up, his eyes gleam, a broad smile spreads on his face. "Oh, it's just exciting," he says, and it's clear to me that "just" here means "very, very." He describes what the bird does as it comes in, how it locks its wings straight out and glides straight in. You can recognize that flight pattern and as soon as you see a bird coming in like that you know it's yours. I realize at one point that you've got to have a fairly settled life style to be a pigeon racer. Because you can't move and take your birds with you. He laughs. And it's true. You can move, but your birds won't. I take the next logical step, which is that if your birds won't move, you probably have to do them all in and start over at a new place, right? Well, you can keep them for breeding stock, but I doubt you could race them again. By the end of the conversation, transient lifestyle aside, I'm ready to get a few birds myself. I really am inspired. I grab a bunch of booklets, I've half decided that I really am going to call my local bunch when I get back. But I won't. It hits me when he talks about all the squab[42] they ate growing up. But when I had the farm I got used to it, so … it's funny how I go around and around with this stuff. We spend more time talking, then walk through the birds as Stan names, describes them, and talks about breed purpose and confirmation. Racers, Czechs, Rollers – all with different looks and characteristics. I'm shocked by some of the Rollers, their aggressiveness, and wonder if they slap like that when you're walking around the pen. Could make for a rather nervewracking hobby …

As I leave Stan, I hear the sincere (if terrifically off key) strains of the National Anthem wafting over from Robinson's Racing Pigs. They started singing it a few days ago (after all, this is a sporting event) and it seems to have caught on. It makes the show last a little longer I guess, and gets people involved, and patriotism is quite in vogue this year … I recorded it the other night, but I record it again. Just in case.

The Together Show band is playing in the Showcase Tent. People have been talking about them all week, and I can see why. They're actually pretty good. A mix of Motown, Santana, and Cubana. They start up a new song, and it's that old Chicago tune that you just can't listen to and keep still. Can't remember the name. "I'm your vehicle, baby, I'll take you anywhere you wanna go, cause I wantcha (wantcha) needya (needya) loveya got – ta have ya chile. Great god in heaven you know I love.…"

Out on the midway is the ever-talking bottle ring toss guy. "Any prize, Any where in the game. Seven rings for a dollar, ring a ding ding ding, get 'em up that thing."

It's late.

Time to go.

This has been a banner day.

Suggested Readings

Emerson, Robert M., Rachel I. Fretz, and Linda L. Shaw. 2011. *Writing Ethnographic Fieldnotes*, 2nd ed. Chicago: University of Chicago Press. Now in its second edition, this book is an already classic guide to writing various kinds of fieldnotes, as well as processing, interpreting, and developing these notes as ethnography.

Sanjek, Roger, ed. 1990. *Fieldnotes: The Making of Anthropology*. Ithaca: Cornell University Press. A classic and critical collection of essays that addresses the deeper nuances and complexities of doing participant observation and writing fieldnotes.

Tedlock, Barbara. 2001. *The Beautiful and the Dangerous: Encounters with the Zuni Indians*, 2nd printing. Albuquerque: University of New Mexico Press. An example of narrative ethnography as per observant participation as outlined in Tedlock's classic article, "From Participant Observation to the Observation of Participation: The Emergence of Narrative Ethnography," which we recommend be read alongside this book (see note 18 for the full reference).

Suggested Websites

Digital Audio Field Recording Equipment Guide – http://www.vermontfolklifecenter.org/archive/res_audioequip.htm A publication of the Vermont Folklife Center, an extensive guide to digital field equipment. Discussion includes information and advice about recorders, microphones, stands, cables, equipment suppliers, and other online and print resources. Two other pages on this same site may also be of interest: (i) "Field Recording in the Digital Age," which includes recommendations for digital recorders (see http://www.vermontfolklifecenter.org/archive/res_digital-age.html); and (ii) "Digital Editing of Field Audio," a great resource on working with digital audio once it is on a computer (see http://www.vermontfolklifecenter.org/archive/res_digitalediting.htm).

Folklife and Fieldwork – http://www.loc.gov/folklife/fieldwork/ A classic guide to documenting folklife and doing fieldwork, posted on the website of the American Folklife Center. Includes discussion of documentary techniques and how to organize results.

Notes

1. Traditional Arts Indiana, "County Fairs," *Field Notes: News from Traditional Arts Indiana* 4, no. 2 (2002): 1.
2. We struggled with how to present these fieldnotes. We wanted, very much, just to present them as they were originally written. And in most cases, we have. But there is a difference between fieldnotes as archived fieldnotes, and fieldnotes as final, published texts. And in some cases, taking excerpts of the polished notes out of the overall collection – as we have done here – also strips them of the context that makes them intelligible –

both intellectually and emotionally. We have thus edited these notes in some places again.

3. Elizabeth Campbell, Lake County Fieldnotes, Indiana County Fairs project, Traditional Arts Indiana and Indiana Historical Society. These notes are currently archived in the Indiana Historical Society Library and Archives.

4. Although reflexivity is not as subject to the charge of "navel-gazing" as it once was, we do want to assert reflexivity is not narcissism; rather, we instead see it as a kind of self-awareness that recognizes the very situated and positioned nature of knowledge, then encourages us to make the connections that are available to us.

5. Excerpted in part from Elizabeth Campbell, "Being and Writing with Others: On the Possibilities of an Ethnographic Composition Pedagogy," PhD diss., Indiana University of Pennsylvania, 2011, 187.

6. See Victor W. Turner and Edward M. Bruner, eds., *The Anthropology of Experience* (Urbana: University of Illinois Press, 1986).

7. See Luke E. Lassiter, *The Power of Kiowa Song* (Tucson: University of Arizona Press, 1998).

8. Timothy J. Cooley and Gregory Barz, "Casting Shadows: Fieldwork is Dead! Long Live Fieldwork!" in *Shadows in the Field: New Perspectives for Fieldwork in Ethnomusicology*, 2nd ed., edited by Gregory Barz and Timothy J. Cooley (Oxford: Oxford University Press, 2008), 13.

9. Bronislaw Malinowski, *Argonauts of the Western Pacific* (London: Routledge, 1922), 24 (emphasis in original).

10. Malinowski, *Argonauts of the Western Pacific*, 25 (emphasis in original).

11. On Boasian influences along these lines, see, for example, Regna Darnell, *And Along Came Boas: Continuity and Revolution in Americanist Anthropology* (Amsterdam: John Benjamins, 1998). On sociological influences, see, for example, W. E. B. Du Bois, *The Philadelphia Negro* (Philadelphia: University of Pennsylvania Press, 1899); Beatrice Potter Webb, *My Apprenticeship* (London: Longmans, Green, and Co., 1926); and Robert and Helen Merrell Lynd, *Middletown: A Study in Modern American Culture* (New York: Harcourt Brace & Company, 1929), respectively.

12. For a more extensive treatment of the development of ethnographic participant observation in sociology and anthropology, see, for example, Arthur J. Vidich and Stanford M. Lyman, "Qualitative Methods: Their History in Sociology and Anthropology," in *The Landscape of Qualitative Research: Theories and Issues*, 2nd ed., edited by Norman K. Denzin and Yvonna S. Lincoln (London: Sage, 2003), 55–129.

13. For an elaboration of this point, see, for example, Luke Eric Lassiter and Elizabeth Campbell, "What Will We Have Ethnography Do?" *Qualitative Inquiry* 16, no. 9 (2010): 757–767.

14. Lassiter and Campbell, *Qualitative Inquiry* 16, no. 9 (2010): 757–767.

15. See, for example, Philippe Bourgois, *In Search of Respect: Selling Crack in El Barrio* (Cambridge: Cambridge University Press, 1995).

16. We do recognize here that "freak show" is a potentially objectionable term. We also recognize that some of the ensuing discussion about "freaks" and "freak shows" may be equally objectionable. For the purposes of this text we have edited the original notes but

tried as much as possible not to change their original content and tone, which reflected the language and experiences of those Beth met on the midway.

17. Barbara Tedlock, *The Beautiful and the Dangerous: Dialogues with the Zuni Indians* (New York: Viking, 1992), xiii.

18. See Barbara Tedlock, "From Participant Observation to the Observation of Participation: The Emergence of Narrative Ethnography," *Journal of Anthropological Research* 47, no. 1 (1991): 69–94.

19. See Barbara Tedlock, "The Observation of Participation and the Emergence of Public Ethnography," in *The Sage Handbook of Qualitative Research*, 3rd ed., edited by Norman K. Denzin and Yvonna S. Lincoln (London: Sage, 2005), 467–481; and "Braiding Narrative Ethnography with Memoir and Creative Nonfiction," in *The Sage Handbook of Qualitative Research*, 4th ed., edited by Norman K. Denzin and Yvonna S. Lincoln (London: Sage, 2011), 331–339. See, too, Elizabeth Campbell, "Being and Writing with Others: On the Possibilities of an Ethnographic Composition Pedagogy," PhD diss., Indiana University of Pennsylvania, 2011.

20. Robert M. Emerson, Rachel I. Fretz, and Linda L. Shaw, *Writing Ethnographic Fieldnotes* (Chicago: University of Chicago Press, 1995), 10.

21. The following discussion relies heavily on Roger Sanjek's important edited volume, *Fieldnotes: The Makings of Anthropology* (Ithaca: Cornell University Press, 1990).

22. Rena Lederman, "Pretexts for Ethnography: On Reading Fieldnotes," in *Fieldnotes*, edited by Roger Sanjek (Ithaca: Cornell University Press, 1990), 88.

23. See Jean E. Jackson, "'I Am a Fieldnote': Fieldnotes as a Symbol of Professional Identity," in *Fieldnotes*, edited by Roger Sanjek (Ithaca: Cornell University Press, 1990), 3–33. See also Roger Sanjek, "A Vocabulary for Fieldnotes," in *Fieldnotes*, 92–121.

24. See Sanjek, "A Vocabulary for Fieldnotes," in *Fieldnotes*, 92–121, from which the following discussion of various types of writing activities conducted in the field draws.

25. Sanjek, "A Vocabulary for Fieldnotes," in *Fieldnotes*, 95–97.

26. Sanjek, "A Vocabulary for Fieldnotes," in *Fieldnotes*, 93–95. See, too, Simon Ottenberg, "Thirty Years of Fieldnotes: Changing Relationships to the Text," in *Fieldnotes*, 139–160.

27. Lederman, "Pretexts for Ethnography," 88.

28. See, for example, Sanjek, "A Vocabulary for Fieldnotes," in *Fieldnotes*, 95–96.

29. Luke Eric Lassiter, *Invitation to Anthropology* (Lanham, MD: AltaMira Press, 2009), 82.

30. See, for example, David Hufford, "Ambiguity and the Rhetoric of Belief," *Keystone Folklore* 21(1): 11–24.

31. James Clifford, "Notes on (Field)notes," in *Fieldnotes*, edited by Roger Sanjek (Ithaca: Cornell University Press, 1990), 47–70.

32. James Clifford, "Notes on (Field)notes," in *Fieldnotes*, edited by Roger Sanjek (Ithaca: Cornell University Press, 1990), 47–70. See, too, James Clifford, "On Ethnographic Authority," *Representations* 1 (1983): 118–146.

33. See, for example, James P. Spradley, *The Ethnographic Interview* (New York: Holt, Rinehart and Winston, 1979), 76.

34. See Clifford, "Notes on (Field)notes," in *Fieldnotes*, edited by Roger Sanjek (Ithaca: Cornell University Press, 1990), 68.

35. See Lederman, "Pretexts for Ethnography," in *Fieldnotes*, edited by Roger Sanjek (Ithaca: Cornell University Press, 1990), 88ff.
36. See Jackson, "'I Am a Fieldnote,'" in *Fieldnotes*, edited by Roger Sanjek (Ithaca: Cornell University Press, 1990), 3–33.
37. There are increasing expectations – among funders, review boards, institutions, and others – that "raw" field materials will be preserved and/or archived in ways that take them out of the immediate control of the ethnographer. This, necessarily, changes how and what researchers write in the field. As we are forced to think more about publication and audiences, something is definitely lost. But something is gained as well: if one is forced to think of one's notes from the outset as inherently public documents, the purpose of those documents changes, along with their form and content. They shift away from purely private accounts, and toward platforms for raising and exploring issues as they emerge.
38. In *Writing Partnerships: Service-Learning in Composition* (Urbana, IL: NCTE, 2000), Thomas Deans explores the difference he sees between "writing with," "writing for," and "writing about" others. The idea of "writing with" resonates for us, as it puts researchers and "the researched" on the most collaborative footing.
39. Excerpted in part from Campbell, "Being and Writing with Others," pp. 218, 228. For an explication of the differences between "writing with," "writing for," and "writing about," see Deans, *Writing Partnerships*.
40. Be aware that we do not mean sequential or singular here. There are bound to be different voices and perspectives in collaborative texts. Those voices and perspectives do not have to agree with each other, but they do have to come together to create some kind of coherent dialogue.
41. See, for example, Deans, *Writing Partnerships*.
42. Young domestic pigeon.

Chapter 5

Interviews and Conversations

Some 20-plus years ago, Eric began working with Kiowa singers on the role and meaning of song in the Kiowa community of southwestern Oklahoma. Ongoing conversations with singers dominated much of the research and writing that went into his first two books, *The Power of Kiowa Song*, which mostly concerned the relationship of Kiowa traditional dance and song; and *The Jesus Road: Kiowas, Christianity and Indian Hymns*, which, co-authored with historian Clyde Ellis and Kiowa singer Ralph Kotay, mostly involved the history and practice of Kiowa-language church hymnody. In both projects, the unique and specific ways in which Kiowa singers communicated knowledge about song – to each other and to outsiders – became critical to the approach and practice of doing ethnographic interviews. We think the following excerpt from *The Power of Kiowa Song* begins to point this out:

> Ernest Doyebi lived down the street from Billy Gene and Shirley. We had met several years earlier when Billy Evans introduced me to him around the drum. A World War II veteran, Ernest had started singing when he returned home after the war. As a young man, he had learned several songs from his father, Nathan Doyebi, a renowned composer and singer of Round Dance songs.

Doing Ethnography Today: Theories, Methods, Exercises, First Edition. Elizabeth Campbell and Luke Eric Lassiter.

One hot August afternoon I walked over to Ernest's house to talk about a new Gourd Dance song he had recently composed. We sat in his bedroom next to an open window – where it would be cool, he said. He sat on the bed, and I sat on a chair next to him. We wiped sweat off our foreheads as we talked. The wind whisked through the window, and the abrasive songs of locusts provided our background music.

We had been talking for several minutes about the role of Gourd Dance songs when I asked (in retrospect, regrettably) about their numbers. "In your estimation, how many Gourd Dance songs are there? Would you have any idea ... "

"Whooh." Ernest released his breath as if I had asked him to ascertain the very number of sounds the locusts had discharged for the past hour.

"... in trying to estimate something like that?"

"I don't know." Ernest paused. "According to the old way back there – time beginning up till now – *aw, man*, I don't know."

"Would you say dozens? Hundreds?"

"*Shoot*. Hundreds." Ernest chuckled, thinking about it. "It's a lot of songs. *Lots* of songs. But we don't sing very many of them. The old songs, they fade away."

"Why is that?"

"I don't know. Some – nobody's singing them. It's like the generation older, a little over a generation, they got songs. They got some *old* songs, but they won't let us have them. If they come out with them [i.e., sing them] and we *sing* them, we can carry them on further down the line. But, like – I know two guys who've got *good* old songs. *Real* old, but they sing for themselves – like I'm sitting here in a room, singing myself – that's all. I heard them boys sing them one time. Boy that's a *beautiful* song. And I couldn't catch it. I didn't have a recorder."[1]

In this particular American Indian community, many value singing as a critical service for the community's social, spiritual, and civic life; singers are needed to give being to a broad range of songs for a variety of events, from Kiowa dances to family memorials to hand game tournaments (a traditional stick game) to church services and other religious ceremonies. Singers are thus incredibly busy, not only with singing at various community, family, or personal events, but also with learning the multitude of old and new songs associated with any particular event, family, or activity. Various groups of singers – who often specialize in particular genres of song – are like extended family groups (and in some cases, being related to each other, they actually are): they meet and sing together regularly, exchanging song and song knowledge with each other in both public and private settings.

While conducting fieldwork in the Kiowa community, Eric spent a great deal of time with singers, especially at "singings," where singers gathered to share a meal together, to sing, and to trade what they knew about old and new songs. The conversations that unfolded at these singings were often vibrant, dynamic, and deeply informative: in addition to singing a song and commenting on the way it "should sound," singers often exchanged information about a song's origin and history, the individual or family to whom it belonged, the occasion(s) for which it should be used (or not used), what its lyrics or contents "said," and other stories associated with its life in the community (which often included humorous narratives about times the song was sung in the wrong setting or for the wrong event).

Singers regularly "made tapes" of these events (i.e., audiotaped recordings done on cassette recorders) to which they could turn for future reference. These they added to other tapes made in similarly public or sometimes more private settings (e.g., a recording of a new song they had "made" – or "caught," as was the terminology among many), on which they commented on a range of knowledge associated with a particular song similar to that voiced during singings. Singers often made copies of their many tapes to distribute to other singers, often reciprocating for the tapes they had received from others.

All of this is to say that singers had their own community-specific way of communicating to each other their song knowledge. So when Eric first started interviewing singers in the early 1990s, he soon noticed that while the interview event could certainly generate long conversations and thick description, the interviews themselves often fell short of capturing the full range and depth of the song knowledge exchanged by singers in events like singings or in communicative exchanges like making tapes. One particular issue concerned the elaboration of the deep emotions often connected to song, voiced sentiments that might surface when singing at community events or at singings, and sometimes even while making tapes, but rarely while talking during interviews. The talk in interviews was often, as one might expect, careful, rational, and measured; the talk surrounding song at, for example, a traditional Kiowa dance, could be filled with impassioned feeling, intense memory, and profound sentiment. Interviews about song, then, prompted very different ways of speaking and very different kinds of information than that elicited by the practice of singing itself. Indeed, many singers were just much more comfortable talking about song on their own terms at a singing or when making a tape than they were answering questions in an interview-structured setting bound by questions originating from Eric's ongoing ethnographic research. As important as interviews were to Eric's projects on Kiowa song, it was critically important for him to recognize, early on, that "people extended meaning through a number of other channels of communication besides the language elicited in the interview event."[2] Moreover, it wasn't enough just to recognize or acknowledge this difference; it was also absolutely critical to engage directly in these other forms of knowledge exchange if he was to apprehend more fully the range and depth of Kiowa song that singers talked about in more formal interviews.[3]

Observing, acknowledging, seeking out, and documenting diverse "channels of communication" is what ethnography is all about, of course. Without the ongoing processes of observant participation, and without direct engagement in these other forms of communicative exchange, any given ethnographic project could be severely limited. In this chapter, we will take up the potentials and pitfalls of the ethnographic interview as a very particular kind of speech event which ethnographers today approach carefully and critically. In many ways, ethnography is incomplete without the many different forms of dialogue that surface around various interview forms, but it is also important to understand that conducting interviews does not, in and of itself, encapsulate the doing of ethnography in any way. Indeed, interviews are only a part – albeit a very important part – of the larger constellation of practices that make ethnography what it is.

Living with Interviews

Turn on the television, read the paper, listen to the radio, surf the web, see a therapist, respond to an opinion poll, apply for a job: we encounter interviews (i.e., the process by which two or more people engage in an information exchange via a process of asking questions and providing answers) everywhere. Whether on talk shows or on the news, at work or at the doctor's office, we use interviews regularly and often to evoke and collect personal history and experience, story and opinion, ideas, expertise, and a broad range of other information. It seems clear, as sociologist David Silverman notes, that we live in "an 'interview society' in which interviews seem central to making sense of our lives."[4] Importantly, we have come to take for granted the idea that the knowledge garnered from interviews is meaningful and, to a certain degree, true – such as when we learn, on a talk show, about "the real person" behind the actress. But that information is constructed as meaningful and true in very specific ways in our society, ways that correspond to our assumptions about what the interview itself is and the kinds of information it is meant to call forth.

Scholars of language and communication have written much about how specific modes of communication – like interviews – index as well as reinforce underlying assumptions about what is considered meaningful and true by members of any given speech community (simply, people who share a common language as well as norms for communicating that language).[5] Sociolinguist and folklorist Charles Briggs, for example, argues that in our mass society a range of implicit, and often unspoken, ideologies about knowledge, language, and speech are at play when we deploy different kinds of interviews in different settings. Among these is the strong belief in the autonomy and freedom of individuals to "speak their minds" and convey their thoughts to others freely and openly. Our ideologies around interviews also construct a clear division of private and public domains, in which presumably autonomous individuals connect to public spheres through particular forms of social interaction ("the interview" being one of these), which, in turn, empower them as citizens. Perhaps most importantly, our ideas about the value of interviews are rooted in the notion of authenticity, the idea that individuals become more fully present and authentic selves via public (and, especially, publicly confessional) discourse. These ideas have deep roots, of course, in both The Enlightenment and modern liberalism; but it certainly hasn't always been – and in many places may still not be – this way. Women, for example, have not always been considered autonomous individuals with fully formed thoughts, who are therefore free to "speak their minds" or to engage others in open dialogue as "true," fully present citizens; the same can also be said for other marginalized groups through time.[6]

That said, interviews as they are understood and used in mass society today tap into the above ideologies in powerful ways. In psychiatric or biographical interviews, for example, interviews are assumed to provide windows into deeper, authentic selves. Interviews are also deployed rhetorically in powerful ways – such as in news stories (and often in ethnographic accounts), where they help to amplify the tacit message of a reporter's (or an ethnographer's) "being there," and thus recording an authentic or "true" account. Interviews are rhetorically powerful in other ways as well. In surveys or polls, for example, when interviews are used to generalize and represent public opinion findings, the interview can be "portrayed not just as ordinary conversations but as carefully structured to elicit inner worlds with minimal intervention and to maximize their value for public discourse."[7]

We do not mean to say here that something is inherently "wrong" with the assumptions and ideologies we are pointing out here. Rather, our aim is to remind readers that there are powerful ideologies about and assumptions behind what is considered meaningful and true and about how interviews evoke meanings and truths, and that these assumptions and ideologies (whatever their form) are deeply historical and cultural. Moreover, they have come to assume such uninterrogated power in contemporary society that if we were to watch news programming about, say, an environmental disaster, most of us would feel quite disconcerted if we did not see or hear from someone "down on the ground," from those people directly affected by the tragedy. Indeed, it just wouldn't feel like a "good," "true" story. In their appeal to our assumptions and ideologies about what is meaningful and true, interviews – talking to the people "there" – generate a sense of the actual experience, authorize knowledge about the larger event, and open up the possibility for emotional connections with those being interviewed. Many of us take this intensely rhetorical process for granted. But not everyone processes language, story, and meaning like this, or at least, not all the time. Take, for instance, Kiowa-language speakers, who often authorize story – especially those associated with language, dance, song, or other tribal traditions – in very different ways: for many Kiowa-speakers, Kiowa-specific stories are not considered "good" or "true" unless they can be directly connected to relationships, which are most often elders who lived in the past. At singings, one of the ways in which Kiowa singers authorized their accounts of an older song's sound and history was to offer statements about from whom they learned the song, usually parents, grandparents, or other elders, whether alive or deceased.

These statements, which often came up after singing the song, were important because authentic learning from parents, grandparents, and other elders transpired not through interview-like question and answer sessions or other such episodes of telling and listening, but by "being with them" in the actual practice of singing, the site where song and its knowledge surfaced. At singings, other singers might question or even challenge another singer about a song's sound or history (as in an interview, albeit with different ideologies at play), but queries that challenged the verity of the song knowledge itself were rarely negotiated: "That's the way my grandfather taught it to me," was an oft-heard, and accepted, response in such cases. Interestingly, though, while differences in song knowledge could be voiced and allowed to co-exist (provided, of course, they could be backed up with such statements), singers might call into question the authenticity of connections to parents, grandparents, and other elders.[8]

Eric had to learn how to approach "singings" as a culturally specific way of introducing, elaborating, and, indeed, negotiating critical song knowledge, knowledge that just did not surface in more conventionally deployed ethnographic interviews. Experiences like these can be very common when doing ethnography, especially when researchers are working with speech communities very different from their own. Hence, why many sociolinguists and other social scientists like Briggs insist that ethnographers approach "the interview" critically, with an eye (or better, an ear) toward the underlying assumptions that we – both ethnographers and the people with whom we work – bring to the interview event. This means, of course, looking out for other ways that people communicate and exchange culturally specific knowledge beyond that which might surface during an interview. But it also means paying very close attention to the complications inherent in the interview event itself.

EXERCISE – ISSUES FOR INTERVIEWS

In earlier Exercises, we explored the complex interplay between being and writing in the field, emphasizing the subjective, positioned, and relational nature of ethnographic work. Thinking about all of that in the context of the ethnographic interview raises issues we have spent considerable time discussing between ourselves and with colleagues (and here we mean all of the many different and differently positioned people with whom we have had the privilege to work). To repeat a point we made earlier, interviews have become so prevalent in contemporary society that we have come to see them as almost natural environments for discovering (or unveiling) true information about people and events. But the interview event itself – with its myriad technical, theoretical, cultural, political, positional, and historical elements – is actually a profoundly complicated thing. In addition to the technical proficiency interviewing requires – and here we mean everything from remembering equipment to collecting high-quality sound to being a generous listener to asking good follow-up questions – there are issues of epistemology, philosophy, and ethics to consider.

Interview preparation involves developing materials and making decisions, and asks us to consider those processes philosophically as well as pragmatically. In ethnography's more classical modes, decisions about whom to interview, what to ask, and how to structure interviews were assumed to belong to the ethnographer him- or herself. But, as with many other elements of contemporary ethnographic practice, the frames for interviews have shifted; today, the above decisions are very likely to be shared, or at least, negotiated. Interview preparations – and the interviews themselves, of course – are also deeply rhetorical constructions that foreground very particular ideas. When we choose whom we will interview, we pick particular points of view; when we choose what to ask, we decide what will become known. As with all fieldwork processes, interviews are situated, particular, and very complex events.

Ideally, we advocate that decisions about whom to interview and what to ask be a collaborative process. But we also recognize that, for reasons of politics and personalities, some of those elements – like, for example, deciding whom to interview – can sometimes be tricky to collaboratively navigate. For that reason, we usually put off making those particular decisions until we are well into the ethnographic project, after project participants have begun to know and trust one another and a shared commitment to the project has begun to emerge. Once they have a strong sense of a project's aims and the value of their own participation, participants often make very valuable suggestions about who should be interviewed and what the focus of interviews should be. In this Exercise, we suggest a series of three discussions that can begin to move your project toward making these complex decisions.

Part 1: Depending upon how your collaboration is structured, engage the following philosophical questions in a small- or large-group discussion:

1. What kind or kinds of knowledge do interviews contribute?
2. To what degree do interviews discover or construct knowledge?
3. To whom does that knowledge belong?
4. At what point is the interview "over"?
5. What do you owe to your "interviewees"?

As much as possible, we try to invite participants to think and talk through these questions with us. Although not everyone wants to engage in academically oriented seminar-style discussion around these issues, the questions above can make for very important and productive conversations among those who are focused on research epistemologies.

Part 2: We assume that most contemporary ethnographic interviews will be more unstructured and emergent than structured, and that interview protocols (i.e., procedures) will thus be quite flexible. But embracing emergence and flexibility does not mean throwing your plans to the wind, or that anything goes. You and project participants will still need to think and talk about what kinds of information you hope to elicit and thus what questions you want to ask. In a large-group discussion, explore the following questions:

1. Reach back to the research questions you developed early on. What do you want to know? What are the large themes you are trying to address? What specific questions (for interviews) can you develop out of your research questions that will help you explore those themes?
2. Do you want all interviewees to answer the same short list of questions? Or would you prefer a long list from which you can pick and choose? Will a diverse collection of personal narratives better suit your aims?
3. What do you want your interviews to do? Share meaning? Describe processes? Collect information? Recall history? Compel action?

Part 3: Discuss, specifically, whom you would like to interview and why. For each person suggested, offer brief biographical information (if known) and describe the particular information or contribution you believe the interview might add to the project.

1. Decide on a process for deciding who will be interviewed, and follow that process through.
2. Discuss, specifically, what you want your interview questions to be for a particular interviewee or groups of interviewees, and then construct the list of questions you will use for each interview. We suggest that you plan to have at least 10 questions for any given interview from which to draw. (Note: although you do want to try to "cover the same ground" in your interviews, you do not have to use exactly the same questions for every interview.) Questions should be specific and to the point, reflecting what it is you want to know and what concepts you would like to explore per

the discussion outlined in Part 2. Again, think about what, exactly, you
want to know. What issues or ideas do you want to explore? What things
are unknown to you about your topic? What new things can you learn
about already-known concepts? As you construct your lists of questions,
consider that:

a. Ethnographers often describe different kinds of questions that they ask
   during ethnographic interviews – such as "descriptive" (which elicit
   information about, for example, places, events, or times), "structural"
   (which elicit information about how people categorize experience,
   based on, for example, values), or "contrast" (which elicit deeper levels
   of meanings based on the comparison of different categories of experience).[9] Remember that different kinds of questions elicit different
   kinds of information, and thus open up different kinds of discussion
   and conversation.

b. Generally, "open-ended questions" will encourage elaboration and
   conversation about a topic; "closed questions" (that elicit a simple or
   one-word response, like "yes" or "no") – which can certainly be used
   – normally do not invite elaboration and conversation about a topic.

c. Finally, think about how your questions are formatted or organized:
   ice-breaker questions can be strategically placed at the interview's start;
   follow-up questions toward the end; and demographic questions
   (which can often elicit rote responses) at the beginning or end, depending on whether you decide to place these when "winding up" or
   "winding down" the interview.

3. Circulate and revise these lists of questions until you are satisfied with
   them as a group.
4. Finally, before starting an actual interview, we find it useful to develop an
   agreed-upon protocol or procedure. The literature on interview procedure
   is extensive (see the Suggested Readings, below, for some exemplary
   examples). Your facilitator or instructor may also have context-specific
   issues or concerns for you to consider, but here are some basic principles
   that we think are important:

   a. Contact your interviewee well in advance (via phone, email, or letter)
      and schedule a date and time for the meeting that is most convenient
      for the interviewee. When scheduling the interview, be very clear about
      your intentions and the goals and purposes of the interview. If you plan
      to record the interview, be sure to mention this up front during initial
      contacts, not when you arrive for the interview. Not everyone will be

comfortable with being recorded (and some may decide against it even at the last minute), so be prepared to take notes without the use of your recorder.

b. Be prompt and courteous, and dress appropriately. (Do not wear flip-flops to an office building, or a suit to a homeless shelter.) Be prepared to engage in conversation before the actual interview event begins. Remember to allow time for setting up and testing your audio, video, or other equipment.

c. If at all possible, select a place (a living room, kitchen table, or sheltered alcove, for example) that is quiet and devoid of sound interference.

d. There is some disagreement about at what point you should dialogue about the project's ethical agreements; for example, about whether interviewees want to be recognized for their contributions or kept anonymous (see chapter 3). We generally advise that this discussion take place before the interview begins, and before the recorder is turned on, so that participants are clear about what they are getting into. In any case, this is a good time for interviewees to review and sign consent forms as per Institutional Review Board (IRB) or other project requirements (see chapter 3).

e. If using a recorder, once the machine is on, record a "tag": state the date and time, your location, your name(s) and have the interviewee(s) state her or his name(s). Your tag should also include a brief statement about the topic or purpose of the interview. (This is incredibly important for large projects should audio or other media recordings get mislabeled or misplaced.) This may also be a good time to restate, "on the record," the rights of the interviewee to stop the recording at any time should they decide to.

f. Begin the interview with "ice-breaker" and descriptive questions, working your way toward deeper, exploratory ones. Many ethnographers choose to begin with demographic or biographical information; others choose to collect this information at the interview's close.

g. There is some disagreement about how long an ethnographic interview should last, but we generally advise no more than an hour. There may be opportunities to do follow-up interviews at a later time; but, in any case, show respect for others' time and look for openings or pauses in conversation to begin winding the interview down.

h. Be absolutely sure to send a follow-up note of thanks. If appropriate, a written thank-you note is ideal.

By the way, for reasons of teamwork and transparency, we think it is reasonable (though it may not always be feasible) for the people you are going to interview to have the questions ahead of time. More importantly, perhaps, if people have time to reflect on interview questions, they will also have time to reflect and to make connections that will likely benefit the project. In a nutshell, once the project's interview questions have been developed, we think it is best to share them.

The Changing Nature of Interviews

Interviews are what sociolinguists call "speech events," particular forms of linguistic and informational exchange that engage participants in a specific kind of communicative act in a specific time and place.[10] Yet even when participants are from the same speech community – a group of speakers who share a similar language and vocabulary, for example – the interview may involve participants from a broad range of different experiences, backgrounds, and circumstances whereby, as Briggs once put it, "the researcher thinks she or he is engaged in an interview, whereas the 'interviewees' believe themselves to be involved in a very different type of speech event."[11] Several researchers have described, for example, how interviewees may inhabit interview roles seen on television or heard on the radio, while the researcher has a very different kind of open-ended ethnographic interview in mind (like those briefly surveyed below); or how rigid interview procedures of "question" and "answer" beget narrow response behaviors that inhibit other forms of talking and relaying information (like telling stories); or how interviewers may inhabit forms of interviewing commonly accepted and oft-used among the middle and upper classes (from which researchers often come), while for interviewees such interviews can carry very different meanings and prompt very different responses across lines of socio-economic class – or, race, ethnicity, religion, age, sexual orientation, and gender for that matter.[12]

Take the issue of age difference and the social roles associated with those differences. Briggs describes a potent example from his own fieldwork with Spanish-speakers in northern New Mexico. "Having entered Córdova unmarried and only nineteen years of age," he writes, "I was not seen as being fully adult. I was similarly ignorant of *Mexicano* culture and of local norms of comportment. Although I spoke Spanish, I was only beginning to learn the local dialect, and I had little grasp of New Mexican Spanish discourse structure. Quite properly (and most fortunately), the Lópezes and other Córdovans took it upon themselves to teach me to behave in accordance with basic *Mexicano* values. Given the community's distrust of

Anglo-Americans, these individuals took this goal quite seriously." Briggs goes on to describe the "pedagogical sessions" in which he learned about Córdova, sessions in which young people are expected to pay close attention and listen. Briggs, of course, could ask questions; but his questioning needed to unfold in ways that respected the status of his elders as teachers, and his status as a learner whose linguistic and cultural competence was still developing. When he tried to ask more conventional interview questions, his hosts regularly pushed these aside, avoiding engagement. "I eventually realized," he writes, "that the Lópezes were implicitly telling me that they could not accept my attempted reversal of the appropriate social roles. If the elders had allowed me to lure them into traditional interviews, they would have accepted a subordinate role in a conversation with a rhetorical incompetent."[13]

Eric remembers similar experiences in his Kiowa song research. Because Eric was interested primarily in the *experience* of singing, he wanted to interview a variety of singers, young and old. Early on, however, both older and younger singers alike questioned him about the need to interview younger singers. Several younger singers (whom he knew well) actually declined to do interviews because they felt uncomfortable being in the "expert" role implied by "doing interviews." That role, many insisted, was more appropriate for elders, who, after all, were more accustomed to responding to questions from anthropologists and other researchers about the expert Kiowa knowledge that elders alone were presumed to possess. Only when younger singers could be assured that they would be engaging in interviews about their own experience of singing and nothing more (such as being asked to make authoritative claims on specific kinds of knowledge reserved for elder singers) did they agree to do the kind of open-ended interview that he sought.[14]

Even then, though, the interview was theoretically under Eric's control – as in many interview events, where the interviewer decides on topics, organizes and structures the interview, creates and asks the questions, and ultimately leads the discussion in desired directions. In many cases, Eric's research interests certainly pushed interviews in those directions. In a few others, however, planned interviews took a very different course as they unfolded, morphing into other community-based forms of communicative exchange: like "making tapes," where the singers themselves assumed more control over the direction and structure of the exchange. One elder singer with whom Eric worked, for example, often brushed aside questions about his experience with singing, and in lieu of doing the arranged interview, regularly insisted that Eric instead help him "make a tape," to record songs he was prepared to sing and the associated knowledge about which he was prepared to talk. In doing so, the singer made sure that Eric "turned off the tape" when talk turned to discussing more private matters like encounter and experience, which for this particular singer was "idle chatter" to fill time between voicing song and its associated knowledge. This process of making tapes put the elder singer in control, where he could communicate the kind of knowledge that he thought the most important for Eric to learn, who, then in his early and mid-twenties, assumed the role of a "younger singer." At the time, Eric was learning how to sing Kiowa songs from this and other elder singers, and younger singers should not ask probing questions, or try to control the structure and direction of knowledge exchange as in an interview; they should listen, and listen carefully.

Such examples illustrate how power relationships – whether they emanate from age or other differences like race, class, gender and the like – can bear on the interview event. We have other examples: during an ethnographic project that involved bikers, for instance, events that Beth framed, arranged, and understood as "interviews" were occasionally re-framed, re-arranged, and re-understood by her consultants as "dates." Many other ethnographers have described similarly complicated experiences with conducting interviews, and have made this point many times before.[15] It is especially important to consider here because, when deployed uncritically, our conventional and taken-for-granted assumptions about the interview and the information we believe it is meant to generate can often take over, directing us down paths that have little to do with openly learning about and with others. In this way these assumptions and ideologies can bear quite negatively on ethnographic and similar research, especially because interviews thus implemented can engage us in a wide range of interpretative mistakes – what Briggs has called "communicative blunders" (i.e., mishaps in communication between those involved in an interview situation) – often without us even knowing that misinterpretations and misunderstandings have unfolded in the process.[16]

With such complexities in the forefront of ethnographic research, contemporary ethnographers see "the interview" in a very different light than they may once have; we can no longer think about interviews as open channels of information flow where knowledge neutrally or uncomplicatedly streams from "informant" to "researcher." Indeed, any interview event is tied to historical, cultural, political, and other social processes far beyond our control; both interviewer and interviewee enter into any given interview event as people, with their unique backgrounds, experiences, assumptions, ideologies, and ethnocentrisms in tow (not to mention their differences in language or language use or meaning). As such, most researchers today are much more flexible in their understanding and use of the interview in ethnographic research; most now couch the interview event as common ground for jointly constructing knowledge, an event in which interviewer and interviewee share in the process of collaboratively crafting shared understandings. Oral historian Valerie Yow, for example, puts it this way:

> In ethnographic research in general and in oral history research specifically, there has been a shift in attitude about the relationship of interviewer to narrator. Formerly, the relationship of researcher (who plays the role of authoritative scholar) to narrator

(who is the passive yielder of data) was once subject to object. In the new view, power may be unequal, but both interviewer and narrator are seen as having knowledge of the situation as well as deficits in understanding. Although the interviewer brings to the interviewing situation a perspective based on research in a discipline, the narrator brings intimate knowledge of his or her own culture and often a different perspective. The interviewer thus sees the work as a collaboration. This is an underlying assumption … [of] "shared authority."[17]

With this underlying assumption of shared authority in mind, we turn now to the contemporary use of interviews in ethnographic fieldwork.

EXERCISE – INTERVIEWS AS CONVERSATIONS

Ethnographic interviews are different from those deployed by journalists, psychologists, police officers, and so on (and each of those kinds of interviews, it is important to remember, are also different from each other). And contemporary ethnographic interviews are different from the ethnographic interviews of an earlier age: today's interviews are much more likely to be understood as mutual constructions or creative collaborations, and less likely to be posed as discovery-oriented question and answer sessions.

We have already made the point that interviews are not neutral or transparent modes of gathering information. To that we also want to add this: in contemporary collaborative work, what emerges out of the interview event is not data, but conversation. We prefer to frame collaboratively situated interviews as conversations rather than "data" for two reasons. First, and perhaps too simply, "data" is a term of science, and conversations are not, *per se*, science; they are better couched in the human arts of understanding, in the humanities. Second, the process of converting human interactions to data (i.e., information presumed to be independent from interpretation) flattens those interactions and strips them of context. These are not minor semantic points; on the contrary, they are primary theoretical issues. The term "data," in our minds, sifts the information out of the information provider, a process that directly contradicts the ethos and aims of collaborative work.[18]

This very brief Exercise asks you to cultivate and practice some of the intellectual and conversational habits that will keep you thinking and acting collaboratively as you conduct interviews.

1. Think of the interviews you conduct as conversations (albeit, with prompts). Rather than ask and answer, or even call and response, think

of these experiences in terms of give and take. Bring your questions to the conversation, and be prepared to answer questions if they are asked of you. Be prepared to go off script, but should you find things going too far afield, find gracious ways to bring the conversation back around.

2. Regularly engage in reflective discussions with a partner about the interviews you conduct. What surprised you? What went well? What did not? What was particularly interesting (or disastrous) about the content of the interview? What was particularly interesting (again, or disastrous) about the interview process? What was the experience like for you?

Framing interviews as conversations rather than data gatherings or other kinds of investigations opens up a project's creative and collaborative possibilities. It also opens up interesting and sometimes tricky methodological concerns. The epistemologically bounded clarity of the traditional "interview" – especially in light of how familiar interviews are in our contemporary "interview culture" – makes the process of doing them seem quite clear: identify research goals, identify questions, identify interviewees, ask questions, go away, analyze (or interpret) transcripts, and present results. The term "conversation" is significantly less bounded, more ephemeral, and, for the purposes of collaborative work, more accurate.

Interviews (and Conversations) in Ethnographic Research

If we assume that conducting interviews in ethnographic research today is ultimately a collaborative venture – one in which knowledge and authority are shared between and among interview participants – then we must also assume that we are doing a very different kind of interview in ethnographic research than in, say, investigative reporting. An investigative reporter may use the interview to collect confidential or secret information (from oft-times anonymous or clandestine informants) that, once gathered, "belongs" to the reporter, to be used in the service of "the story" (in normal circumstances, both interviewer and interviewee understand and accept this). A host of theoretical, ethical, and pragmatic concerns and issues – as well as legal consequences – grow out of those assumptions, of course; concerns and issues that are unique to the history, culture, and politics of what we know to be investigative reporting.

The same is true for ethnography. In the context of ethnographic research, very different assumptions underline the interview event in ways that are quite different from other forms of interviewing. In theoretical terms – terms expressed by Yow above – the knowledge produced in an interview is always collective, emergent in the context of dialogue. Knowledge amassed by an ethnographer is thus intimately tied to conversations encountered in the fields in which she works. Ethnographic knowledge does not exist independently from those conversations; it is intimately tied to them. This means, of course, that knowledge collected in an interview event, in particular, is never the ethnographer's alone; it belongs to multiple parties. As his Kiowa consultants often reminded Eric, the song knowledge that he collected and learned – from interviews, singings, the process of making tapes, or otherwise – should never be passed off as his alone (singers insisted, for example, that they be cited as sources of knowledge just like any other source of knowledge – a book, for example).[19]

While a theoretical concern, this is also an obviously ethical and, importantly, legal issue. In oral history research, for instance, researchers generally understand that in terms of copyright, any recorded interview does not "belong" to the interviewer alone; legally, the interviewee holds copyright of a narrated account until informed consent is provided by the interviewee(s) to the interviewer.[20] But even then, the narrator's account is not entirely "owned" by the interviewer; many contemporary researchers and archivists may still consider it jointly created and authored, and proceed accordingly when dealing with interviews as a part of a larger ethnographic research project.[21] Keeping this idea of jointly authored interviews in mind, then, it may be easier to appreciate why the theoretical, ethical, and legal understandings of the ethnographic interview are oftentimes very much at odds with conventional notions (and at times forced conditions) of informed consent – often derivative of IRB requirements that stem from positivist assumptions of conducting research (see the discussion accompanying the Exercise in chapter 3 titled "Ethics, IRBs, and Other Subjects") – which may "require" that so-called subjects be engaged and represented anonymously. As discussed in chapter 3, most ethical codes stipulate that ethnographic consultants have the "right" to be recognized (or not, should they wish to remain anonymous) for their contributions to ethnographic knowledge, which is much more in line with the current theoretical, ethical, and legal thinking behind interviews as a collaborative, jointly constructed venture.

We will come back to the broader implications of these issues when we discuss the process of moving the interview event to interview text (such as in transcripts, below). But for now, we think it especially important to establish that doing ethnographic research necessitates that we first and foremost begin with thinking in very particular ways about ethnographic interviews (theoretically, ethically, legally) as being very different from other kinds of interviews (e.g., investigative reporting); which should, in turn, influence how we go about *doing* these interviews – that is, with actual people, who possess expertise and proficiency; outlooks and mindsets; opinions and agendas; wants and needs; feelings and sentiments (just like us).

When it comes to actually doing ethnographic interviews, one can find a plethora of books about ethnographic interviews and interviewing.[22] As ethnographers today hail from many different disciplines, they may use different kinds of interviews and interviewing techniques, including structured, semi-structured, and unstructured. Structured interviews generally involve interview events in which an interviewer(s) poses the same set of questions to different people within the context of the same research project (as in a survey, for example); narration or conversation that diverges from these pre-established questions is discouraged. Semi-structured interviews proceed from an established set of questions (as in structured interviews), though narration or conversation that opens new lines of inquiry is valued and encouraged. Unstructured interviews generally involve more open-ended conversations in which particular kinds of knowledge are sought from specific interviewees (as in an oral or life history interview, for example). In structured interviews, control and authority rest mostly with the researcher; in semi-structured and unstructured interviews, control and authority are more likely to be shared.

For obvious reasons, semi-structured and unstructured interviews are more common in ethnographic research, where ethnographers must engage both formal and informal communicative exchanges in the context of doing fieldwork. When conducting his Kiowa song research, for example, Eric frequently recorded brief "informal interviews" when conversations during a meal, while traveling, or when visiting with others turned to issues having to do with Kiowa song. (He was well known among Kiowa singers for having a recorder available at a moment's notice should the conversation turn.) More "formal interviews," however, often transpired at a prescribed time and place; the interview prompted by open-ended questions originating from his evolving ethnographic interests in Kiowa song. As in most unstructured interviews, Eric's questions served as a springboard for discussion, which, in turn, often led in unexpected directions originating new questions to be explored in future formal and informal interviews.

Ethnographers may also use focus or group interviews (in which groups of people are encouraged to respond to questions or ideas and openly dialogue about a particular issue or set of issues), as well as telephone and even electronic interviewing. Electronic or virtual interviewing, in particular, is increasingly common in ethnographic research, in which researchers may use media like email, online discussion forums, video conferencing, and other communication technologies to conduct interviews.[23] Communications studies scholar Annette Markham, for example, completed an entire ethnographic project online, conducting ethnographic interviews virtually. In her book, *Life Online: Researching Real Experience in Virtual Space*, Markham writes that it was difficult to know people "beyond the words I see scrolling up my own screen. [But] this does not mean the interview is less interesting. Through their words and through my interaction with them, I could sense joy, anger, passion, bitterness, happiness. In fact, I was surprised and impressed by the intensity of the conversations."[24]

Though Markham conducted her interviews textually, virtual interviews can just as easily be conducted through voice-over-IP and instant messaging services, like Skype. Virtual or otherwise, ethnographers may further distinguish the kinds of interviews implemented in various projects – such as narrative, oral history, or biographical interviews (which emphasize collecting narratives of experience); descriptive or fact-finding interviews (which emphasize elaborating knowledge of a particular topic or issue); and constructivist, co-theoretical, or hermeneutic interviews (which emphasize exploring the deeper or philosophical meanings of a particular topic or issue).[25] In Eric's research on Kiowa song, he interviewed singers about their individual experience and history with singing; about their knowledge of particular songs or Kiowa traditions; and about their perspectives on and philosophies of song, respectively.

Such interviews, of course, can be organized successively or sequentially: ethnographers may begin their projects with narrative and descriptive interviews, following up these with constructivist or hermeneutic interviews as new understandings emerge and a project develops. This approach is particularly common in linguistic or semantic analysis, where ethnographers may scaffold interviews to better understand the taxonomic structure and negotiated meanings of language in use in a particular social setting. In any case, during the process of conducting multiple and sequential interviews, ethnographers may regularly use so-called member validation or participant checking (i.e., when a researcher checks or validates her or his developing comprehension of a particular topic or issue with the interviewee).[26] Such corroboration, perhaps obviously, helps to build active dialogue and collaborative participation into the interview process, inviting feedback, commentary, and even criticism from interviewees, who may, of course, differ in their interpretations of a given topic or issue.

Participant checking is sometimes framed as a kind of triangulation (i.e., examining or confirming received information from multiple positions or perspectives), but it can be much more complicated and multidimensional than this. In contemporary practice, participant checking can often push interview events beyond their narrow confines and into more reciprocal, discursive, and conversational communicative spaces, in which both ethnographer(s) and their consultants or "conversational partners" are asking questions, offering responses, and together charting collaborative interpretations of phenomena. As any given ethnographic project progresses, this process can also grow into dialogic editing, which involves discussion of developing ethnographic texts (an issue that we will cover in the next chapter), which, in turn, can provide ways into even deeper co-theoretical discussion and understanding. Folklorist Glenn Hinson, for example, writes about this process in his ethnography *Fire in My Bones: Transcendence and the Holy Spirit in African American Gospel*:

> Throughout the process of writing, consultants in the church have read, commented upon, and contributed to my observations. When they have pointed errors in logic or interpretation, I have made the suggested changes. When they have suggested issues that deserved elaboration, I have tried to elaborate. And when they have offered anecdotal assessments that brought new insights, I have tried to incorporate the insights – and often the anecdotes themselves – into the text. Together, we have tried to present the(ir) lived logic of sanctified meaning.
>
> This logic charts a fullness that might never have been evident had the saints not repeatedly grounded our conversations in the experiences that set their world apart. Every testimony told of spiritual encounter; every story suggested the taken-for-grantedness of grace; every song alluded to epiphany. These references, in turn, opened the door to a new domain of understanding.[27]

Opening new domains of understanding through dialogue and conversation, of course, is precisely what ethnography is all about.

A related form of discursive exchange concerns the opening up of not just new domains of understanding, but new domains of cooperative action as well. Many ethnographers and their ethnographic collaborators may come to experience interview events as potential sites for augmenting community or civic involvement, where the consciousness-raising aspects of collaborative knowledge production may lead them to take action together. In the Other Side of Middletown project, for example, several of the students, as a direct result of their interviews and ongoing conversations with their consultants, were moved to civic engagement and community action around race relations in Muncie.[28] In her ethnography *Intercultural Utopias*, anthropologist Joanne Rappaport describes a similar process whereby her ethnographic work with the Regional Indigenous Council of Cauca (or CRIC), a group of indigenous activists in Colombia's Cauca region, led to collaborative dialogue and activist work that extended beyond the use of formal interviews and informal conversations:

> In my previous experience in Tierradentro … and in the Pasto community of Cumbal on the Colombia-Ecuador border … I took ethnographic dialogue to consist of formal interviews and informal conversations, which were precisely the tools I first used to set about learning about indigenous intellectuals in millennial Cauca. But when I entered into dialogue with CRIC activists, I was swiftly drawn by them into a broader array of conversational venues. During the first research season, I sought out Jesús Enrique (Chucho) Piñacué, Susana's brother and at the time president of CRIC (he is now a national senator). Chucho informed me that if I was to conduct research in CRIC, I would be expected to collaborate in community projects; he was referring

particularly to my expertise in historical research, which would be of use in a number of localities. When I first became involved with CRIC's bilingual education program and, to a lesser extent, with a history project in northern Cauca, I swiftly learned that dialogue with activists did not occur only on a one-on-one basis, nor could I confine my fieldwork to traditional forms of participant observation, where "participant" meant accompanying the activities I was observing and not intervening in them. The collaboration that the activists sought involved expanding my venues of dialogue to include workshops, in which I not only participated but occasionally acted as a facilitator, work on joint research projects with CRIC personnel, engagement in exegetical meetings with the research team and with CRIC's bilingual education program, and the exchange of commentary on written work. In other words, I was enjoined to become an actor in the process I was studying....[29]

These examples illustrate how dialoging with ethnographic partners can lead ethnographers into domains of action – or pull them swiftly into action, as in Rappaport's case – even when ethnographers may begin their work with only formal interviews and informal conversations in mind. Such are the collaborative and dialogic contexts in which we often find ourselves doing ethnography today. But in some kinds of ethnography, particularly in forms of participatory action research, ethnographic interviews can be used even more deliberately to connect people, research, and action from the outset. The approach is sometimes called cooperative inquiry, a participatory, dialogic method that may begin with an identification of some problem – social or otherwise – which researchers and community partners seek to address or solve through first collaboratively identifying research questions, and then cooperatively researching those questions with the explicit intention of solving or addressing the identified problem. In many cases, research participants are mobilized to conduct interviews to elaborate the nature of the problem, to raise consciousness among participants, and to co-develop strategies for change.[30]

Not all ethnographic projects, of course, move in these directions. But it is important to know that, in practice, doing ethnographic interviews – from the earliest biographical or fact-finding to the more deeply hermeneutic, like that relayed by Hinson, to the more activist or participatory, like that relayed by Rappaport – rarely advances in quite the same way as the more stereotypical question/response kind of event many imagine when they think "interview." In the context of an extended ethnographic project, "interviews" are best thought of as ongoing conversations: evolving, unstructured exchanges of concepts and ideas that, in practice, characteristically lead ethnographers and their consultants in unexpected directions and into new domains of understanding, and perhaps new domains of collective action. Because of this dialogic process, many ethnographers are therefore more comfortable with calling the wide range of open-ended interviews in which they engage in any particular ethnographic project "conversations" or "dialogues" – because this is exactly what they are.[31]

Aside from calling something what it is – as well as endeavoring to be more consistent with the underlying epistemologies of ethnographic research today – casting interviews in more conversational and discursive terms further underlines the range of forms, contexts, and purposes of communicative exchange now at work in ethnographic research.[32]

In the end, though, interview events are only *one* of the many communicative channels that ethnographers encounter while doing fieldwork: communication achieves (and constructs) meaning in multiple ways, ways that interviews may not fully address (as Eric's Kiowa song research illustrates).[33] And here we come full circle: again, the knowledge that we collect from talking with people is only part – albeit a rather large one – of the work we do as ethnographers: interviews cannot stand for ethnography, which also requires us to participate, engage, observe, write, collaborate, and perhaps even act for change.

EXERCISE – TALKING ABOUT TRANSCRIPTS

We have reached an especially critical juncture in the collaborative process. Before we get to the actual Exercise, we think it is important to explain why, specifically, we think this is so important.

Elsewhere, we (particularly Eric in his *Chicago Guide to Collaborative Ethnography*) have argued for extending ethnography's dialogic metaphor into its textual practice by bringing the project's evolving texts back into the field and placing them at the center of a deepening conversation. This, too, is more complicated than it sounds. Because so many of the texts that rise out of ethnographic projects are print-based, it is important to remember that texts are connected to literacies, which vary in both kind and degree across contexts. There are also questions of time and desire to consider; not everyone has time or even wants to read, comment on, or rewrite the things that we write. Finally, in particular contexts and among specific people, different kinds of texts seem to provoke varied levels of interest and response. In the Lake County Fair Project (discussed in the last chapter), a number of the carnival workers wanted access to Beth's notes, but few of the Fair exhibitors did. In Eric's work in Kiowa country, many participants wanted to read and comment on recording or interview transcripts, and then to receive copies of the revised transcript for their own collections (or for distribution to others). In the study of university-school collaborations mentioned in chapter 2, very few were interested in the transcripts, but some were very interested in the project's evolving report drafts.

Raising the university-school project here brings up an important consideration: beyond the degree to which participants are willing and able to engage in conversations around project texts, a project's parameters and goals will also determine how much influence those reviews and conversations can reasonably exert. What may be appropriate in documentary, creative, or community development projects, for example, may not be appropriate in evaluative projects that aim to assess or improve a particular policy or initiative. As we have tried to make clear throughout this text, there is no one way to describe or "do" collaboration; again, contemporary collaborative work is profoundly particular. Although we believe that conversations around shared texts are a critical component of contemporary ethnographic practice, the extent to which you enact that component will depend on you, your project, your participants, your goals, your institutional contexts ... well, we have been through all of that.

However you decide to share project texts, it is important to keep in mind the philosophical frame behind this desire to "extend the dialogic metaphor" into textual practice. It is partly concerned with ethics, a move toward equity and fairness. But in the context of collaborative work, it is also an important methodological concern, the next move in a deepening conversation that brings us closer to both difference and understanding. In its best iteration, sharing project texts is not a bureaucratic move that seeks approval, nor is it only an act of fairness or generosity; sharing written materials can open up new avenues of conversation that can lead to important and often unexpected understandings, and to deepened relationships.

It seems that we increasingly live in societies that do not make room for meaningful conversations across difference. Although globalization and digital technologies allow us to encounter – or, perhaps better, consume – difference more now than we ever have, much of the time we only talk with people who are like us; we rarely engage in conversations with those who are different from us, whether in terms of class, race, ethnicity, politics, religion, profession, or background. But ethnography offers us – and by "us" here we mean both ethnographers and project participants – real opportunities to engage each other's differences. It is one thing to sit in an interview and ask questions about difference; it is another thing entirely to engage those with whom we differ in meaningful conversation about those differences. These conversations – not questions, or answers, or small talk but *conversations* – can take us into challenging and difficult territory that can require negotiation. But with all of the conversations and negotiations you have already engaged – around personal and locational possibilities, ethical codes and IRBs, observant participation and meaningful engagement, writing in the field, designing interviews, and so on – you have good practice. The skills, insights, and relationships you developed in those processes will carry you through these conversations ahead.

Speaking of which, if you have been thinking ahead, it has probably occurred to you that sharing project texts could invite project participants to edit, alter, or delete what they have said or contributed. Without beating around the bush, it is true; they most definitely could. And they will. For some, this is highly controversial. But again, because the ethnography we have in mind aims to creatively and constructively build relationships and understanding rather than to investigate or discover information or knowledge, this is not a major concern. (If you are looking for a discussion topic that will fire everybody up, by the way, the aims of ethnography is one we highly recommend.)

Our thinking on this stance has evolved significantly over the years. When we first started out, we operated within theoretical paradigms that emphasized anti-colonialism and representational equity. Back then, we accommodated requests for deletions on purely ethical and moral grounds: the humanity of our participants took precedence over our research goals, so anything they wanted taken out got taken out. (After all, we do the same when we are writing and producing *our* texts; why not extend that to others?) That was a satisfactorily righteous position, but the issue itself is really much more complicated. Beyond the charge traditionalists make of interfering with the science of the thing, or of editing out unflattering information, or of giving participants too much control over research outcomes, there are very real problems of masking to consider, about which a number of scholars, feminist in particular, have written quite eloquently.[34]

Although participants have occasionally asked us to strike their words and ideas from the record, it has not happened often. And when it has happened, it has always been for very good reasons. People have let their guards down during interviews/conversations and said things about friends and family that they have later regretted; when they asked us to strike those things from the texts, we did. In a few cases, people have later worried about the professional prudence of some comments; if they have asked us to strike those elements from the record, we have. Beth once interviewed someone about an arts tradition, but he ended up talking about a local controversy (connected with that tradition) that he had never talked about before. Several days later, he called, said he was concerned about repercussions, and asked her to delete the entire record. It was almost painful (the interview really was that good); but, she wiped the transcript from her computer, destroyed the recording, and mailed it (along with the signed consent form) back to him.

Although these might seem on the surface like setbacks, our experience has been that these deletions have almost always resulted in even deeper conversations. Real trust has come out of our willingness to actually do what we have said we will do, and that has kept the doors open for future conversations. And then there are the deletions themselves. One of our sagest professors used to say that when people want to strike parts of transcripts, they are telling you something important. In fact, they are saying as much – and often, much more – than what they originally said. He was right: What we have gained from what people have wanted us to take out has been, almost without exception, much more valuable than what we have lost.

Thank you for bearing with this extended discussion. You will be pleased to know that the Exercise itself is fairly straightforward. Here is what we recommend for transcribing an interview:

1. Think ahead about the equipment you will need to transcribe the interview. These days, downloading an audio recording from the machine to a computer via USB or FireWire is a relatively simple and straightforward process. Provided your machine uses audio formats that are not proprietary (see the Interlude on equipment in chapter 4), you can use a variety of software programs to play your recording back: some are free to download, like Audacity (http://audacity.sourceforge.net/). But whatever software you choose, make sure it has basic playback controls; chief among these is the ability to slow a recording down so you can effectively transcribe it without having to constantly stopping, rewinding, and playing a recording. Most advanced sound programs can interface with now widely available USB or FireWire foot pedals (also called "foot controls" or "transcriptions pedals"), which can be used to start and stop, rewind, and fast-forward recordings without the user having to remove her or his hands from the keyboard.
2. After the interview is finished, transcribe it word for word. Do this as quickly as possible. It will be easier for you to transcribe, for your interview partner to recall, and for you both to discuss if you do not let more than a few days to a week go by. Once you have finished with the transcription, send it to your interview partner (i.e., interviewee) and set a

date (ideally, no more than a week or two out) to discuss the transcript. Ask your interview partner to highlight or circle, and make brief notes on:
- issues that are very important
- issues she would like to expand or clarify
- issues that could be misunderstood or misinterpreted
- questions or additional issues the interview transcript raises
- mistakes in the information or transcript.
3. Go through the interview transcript yourself and make the same highlights and notes.
4. Come together with your interview partner and use the above questions as a guide for a new conversation. Be sure to record and transcribe this conversation as well, and to discuss it again.

Suggested Readings

Briggs, Charles. 1986. *Learning How to Ask: A Sociolinguistic Appraisal of the Role of the Interview in Social Science Research*. Cambridge: Cambridge University Press. A classic guide on the nuances and complexities of learning how to ask questions in the context of doing ethnographic fieldwork.

Powers, Willow Roberts. 2005. *Transcription Techniques for the Spoken Word*. Lanham, MD: AltaMira Press. Elaborates many of the techniques and methods involved in transcription, as well as many of the ethical and social contexts in which transcriptions surface. A very helpful guide for both beginning and seasoned transcriptionists.

Rappaport, Joanne. 2005. *Intercultural Utopias: Public Intellectuals, Cultural Experimentation, and Ethnic Pluralism in Columbia*. Durham: Duke University Press. An innovative ethnography that builds on conversations between the author and indigenous activists in Colombia's Cauca region.

Tedlock, Dennis, and Bruce Mannheim, eds. 1995. *The Dialogic Emergence of Culture*. Urbana: University of Illinois Press. A classic collection of essays exploring how language and cross-cultural understandings are created and recreated via ethnographic dialogue.

Yow, Valarie Raleigh. 2005. *Recording Oral History: A Guide for the Humanities and Social Sciences*, 2nd ed. Lanham, MD: AltaMira Press. An extensive and thorough discussion of interviews in oral history and ethnographic research. Includes several helpful discussions on kinds of interviews, ethical and legal issues, selecting narrators/interviewees, interpersonal relations, creating research questions, organizing and carrying out interviews, analysis and interpretation, and publishing results.

Suggested Websites

Interviewing Guidelines – http://oralhistory.library.ucla.edu/interviewGuidelines.html Developed by the Center for Oral History Research at UCLA, this site lays out some basic information for doing oral history and ethnographic interviews, including equipment and audio recording tips, interviewing techniques, and interviewing tips.

Indexing and Transcribing Your Interviews – http://www.loc.gov/vets/transcribe.html A brief description from the American Folklife Center's Veterans History Project that details information about indexing (or "logging") and transcribing interviews. Links to the larger project and advice for carrying out interviews are also available on the site.

Smithsonian Folklife and Oral History Interviewing Guide – http://www.folklife.si.edu/resources/pdf/interviewingguide.pdf A freely available online PDF of the 2003 publication. A great resource.

Notes

1. Excerpted from Luke Eric Lassiter, *The Power of Kiowa Song: A Collaborative Ethnography* (Tucson: University of Arizona Press, 1995), 151–152.
2. Lassiter, *The Power of Kiowa Song*, 59.
3. See Lassiter, *Power of Kiowa Song*, 57–65.
4. David Silverman, *Interpreting Qualitative Data: Methods of Analyzing Talk, Text and Interaction*, 3rd ed. (London: Sage, 2006), 30. See also Paul Atkinson and David Silverman, "Kundera's Immortality: The Interview Society and the Invention of the Self," *Qualitative Inquiry* 3, no. 3 (1997): 304–325.
5. See, for example, Michael Agar, *Language Shock: Understanding the Culture of Conversation* (New York: Quill, 1994); Nancy Bonvillain, *Language, Culture, and Communication: The Meaning of Messages*, 6th ed. (Upper Saddle River, NJ: Prentice Hall, 2010); Charles Briggs, *Learning How to Ask: A Sociolinguistic Appraisal of the Role of the Interview in Social Science Research* (Cambridge: Cambridge University Press, 1986); Charles Briggs, with others, "Anthropology, Interviewing, and Communicability in Contemporary Society," *Current Anthropology*, vol. 48, no. 4 (2007): 551–580; Dell Hymes, *"In Vain I Tried to Tell You": Essays in Native American Ethnopoetics* (Philadelphia: University of Pennsylvania Press, 1981); and Muriel Saville-Troike, *The Ethnography of Communication: An Introduction*, 3rd ed. (Oxford: Blackwell Publishing, 2003). For more that problematizes the interview in social science research in particular, see, for example, Atkinson and Silverman's "Kundera's Immortality"; Andrea Fontana and James H. Frey, "The Interview: From Neutral Stance to Political Involvement," in *The Sage Handbook of Qualitative Research*, 3rd ed., edited by Norman K. Denzin and Yvonna S. Lincoln (London: Sage, 2005), 695–727; and Jennifer Platt, "The History of the Interview," in *Handbook of Interview Research: Context and Method*, edited by Jaber F. Gubrium and James A. Holstein (London: Sage, 2002), 33–54.

6. See Briggs, "Anthropology, Interviewing, and Communicability in Contemporary Society."

7. Briggs, "Anthropology, Interviewing, and Communicability in Contemporary Society," 555.

8. For more on the rhetoric surrounding how song knowledge is authorized among Kiowa singers, see Lassiter, *Power of Kiowa Song*, 129–186.

9. See James P. Spradley, *The Ethnographic Interview* (New York: Holt, Rinehart and Winston, 1979).

10. See, for example, Dell Hymes, *Foundations in Sociolinguistics: An Ethnographic Approach* (Philadelphia: University of Pennsylvania Press, 1974).

11. Hymes, *Foundations in Sociolinguistics*, 39.

12. Hymes, *Foundations in Sociolinguistics*, 56–59. See also Fontana and Frey, "'The Interview: From Neutral Stance to Political Involvement."

13. Briggs, *Learning How to Ask*, 57–58.

14. Cf. Lassiter, *Power of Kiowa Song*, 153–157.

15. See note 5.

16. Briggs, *Learning How to Ask*.

17. Valarie Raleigh Yow, *Recording Oral History: A Guide for the Humanities and Social Sciences*, 2nd ed. (Walnut Creek: AltaMira Press, 2005), 1–2.

18. Excerpted in part from Elizabeth Campbell, "Being and Writing with Others: On the Possibilities of an Ethnographic Composition Pedagogy," PhD diss., Indiana University of Pennsylvania, 2011, 144.

19. See Dennis Tedlock and Bruce Mannheim, eds., *The Dialogic Emergence of Culture* (Urbana: University of Illinois Press).

20. See John A. Neuenschwander, *A Guide to Oral History and the Law* (Oxford: Oxford University Press, 2009).

21. See Yow, *Recording Oral History*, 121–156.

22. Ethnographers across the social sciences and humanities problematize the interview in varying ways, of course, and offer differing acknowledgements of the inherent problems of the ethnographic interview as well as its possibilities in ethnographic research. In addition to Gubrium and Holstein's *Handbook of Interview Research*, which provides a range of approaches and perspectives on the interview and the larger "interview society" in which we live, see, for example, Steinar Kvale, *Doing Interviews* (London: Sage, 2007); Steinar Kvale and Svend Brinkman, *Interviews: Learning the Craft of Qualitative Research Interviewing*, 2nd ed. (London: Sage, 2009); James A. Holstein and Jaber F. Gubrium, eds., *Inside Interviewing: New Lenses, New Concerns* (London: Sage, 2003); Stephen L. Schensul, Jean J. Schensul, and Margaret D. LeCompte, *Essential Ethnographic Methods: Observations, Interviews, and Questionnaires* (Walnut Creek, CA: AltaMira Press, 1999); and James P. Spradley, *The Ethnographic Interview* (New York: Holt, Rinehart, and Winston, 1979). Scholars and practitioners of oral history, in particular, offer a range of critical and thoughtful analyses of the use of interviews in their craft. In addition to Yow's *Recording Oral History*, see, for example, Thomas L. Charlton, Lois E. Meyers, and Rebecca Sharpless, eds., *Handbook of Oral History* (Lanham, MD: AltaMira Press, 2006); Robert Perks and Alistair Thomson, eds., *The Oral History Reader* (London: Routledge,

1998); and Donald A. Ritchie, *Doing Oral History: A Practical Guide* (Oxford: Oxford University Press, 2003).

23. See, for example, Annette N. Markham and Nancy K. Baym, eds., *Internet Inquiry: Conversations about Method* (London: Sage, 2009).

24. Annette N. Markham, *Life Online: Researching Real Experience in Virtual Space* (Walnut Creek, CA: AltaMira Press, 1998), 71.

25. For more in-depth discussions about these and other types of interviews, see Note 22.

26. See, for example, Spradley, *The Ethnographic Interview*.

27. Glenn Hinson, *Fire in My Bones: Transcendence and the Holy Spirit in African American Gospel* (Philadelphia: University of Pennsylvania Press, 2000), 324–325.

28. See, for example, Elizabeth Campbell and Luke Eric Lassiter, "From Collaborative Ethnography to Collaborative Pedagogy: Reflections on the Other Side of Middletown Project and Community-University Research Partnerships," *Anthropology & Education Quarterly* 41, no. 4 (2010): 370–385.

29. Joanne Rappaport, *Intercultural Utopias: Public Intellectuals, Cultural Experimentation, and Ethnic Pluralism in Colombia* (Durham: Duke University Press, 2005), 88.

30. See, for example, John Heron, *Co-Operative Inquiry: Research into the Human Condition* (London: Sage, 1996); Peter Reason, ed., *Human Inquiry in Action: Developments in New Paradigm Research* (London: Sage, 1988); and Peter Reason and Hilary Bradbury, eds., *The Sage Handbook of Action Research: Participative Inquiry and Practice* (London: Sage, 2008).

31. See, for example, Kevin Dwyer, *Moroccan Dialogues: Anthropology in Question* (Prospect Heights, IL: Waveland Press, 1987); Dennis Tedlock, *The Spoken Word and the Work of Interpretation* (Philadelphia: University of Pennsylvania Press, 1983); and Tedlock and Mannheim, *The Dialogic Emergence of Culture*.

32. In some ways this shift in terminology also marks a distancing from interviews as commonly defined and deployed in more positivist-oriented research (both qualitative and quantitative), which may oftentimes model the interview event as a one-dimensional tool for just "gathering data" (and not for, among other things, exploring meaning discursively and collaboratively). The casting of interviews as sites for ongoing dialogue, conversation, and discussion is often attributed to the rise of postmodernism and feminism in the social sciences and humanities, the former accentuating, among other things, the deconstruction of taken-for-granted research epistemologies; the latter stressing, among other things, structures of inequity inherent in all forms of communication (see, for example, Fontana and Frey, "The Interview: From Neutral Stance to Political Involvement," 709–712). But the underpinnings of these ideas are much older, finding their roots (if not their exact phrasing) in the humanistic (and honestly, more honest) approaches to doing fieldwork common among late nineteenth- and early twentieth-century humanists who, albeit harboring what are now considered dated theoretical assumptions with serious shortcomings, nevertheless cast their ethnographic projects in much more humanistic and peopled terms (see herein chapter 1; for more on this, see Luke Eric Lassiter, *The Chicago Guide to Collaborative Ethnography* (Chicago: University of Chicago Press, 2005), 25–47). In any case, thanks to the rise of more contemporary interpretive approaches (as ushered in by Geertz, for example) and, indeed, the more

recent developments of postmodernism and feminism, these ideas are much more common than they once were. And ethnographers are, consequently, much more open to framing ethnographic dialogues as ways to deepen individual ethnographic projects that, in turn, deepen the broader purposes of the larger ethnographic project to understand people in all of their complexities.

33. See Hymes, *Foundations in Sociolinguistics*.
34. See, for example, Judith Stacey, "Can There Be a Feminist Ethnography?" *Women's Studies International Forum* 11, no. 1 (1988): 21–27.

Chapter 6

Inscriptions: On Writing Ethnography

The various ethnographic projects with which we have been involved – many of which we have discussed in the preceding pages – have engendered very diverse kinds and styles of ethnographic forms (an admittedly problematic term we use to describe the vast range of texts, productions, actions, and new projects that emerge out of ethnographic work). Although we acknowledge that ethnographic forms are not always or necessarily text-based, writing has always been central to our own ethnographic practice. We do want to point out that others are attending more and more to ethnography's dialogic and performative forms; still, because so much of the collaborative promise we have seen in ethnographic work has concerned ethnographic writing – especially writing that moves between ethnographic collaborators – our primary focus in this final chapter is on literal forms of inscription – "texts" written on some form of "page."

These "texts" and "pages," however, are not ends in and of themselves; rather, they are part of a recursive, collaborative process. Wherever possible, we have tried to engage ethnographic writing that works – albeit, very differently from project to project – between us and the people with whom we work. In the applied ethnographic project on university-school collaborations we briefly described in chapter

Doing Ethnography Today: Theories, Methods, Exercises, First Edition. Elizabeth Campbell and Luke Eric Lassiter.

2, for example, we generated periodic written summaries of our ongoing findings, and, in the end, produced a rather large and involved written report that included our analysis of the project's collaboration between universities, outreach professors, school teachers, and local schools. Given the role of original interview transcripts in this research, the report also included those transcripts. Although several of the interviewees had reviewed and in a few cases asked for changes (the reasons for which we have explored in the last chapter), in the end, project participants were minimally engaged in the actual writing of the project's report. Although many of our interviewees presumably read the transcripts, periodic summaries, and final reports that we generated (and perhaps even integrated our findings into their understandings and practices as it related to their work), the funders and organizers of the university-school collaborations (on both federal and state levels) were, ultimately, the intended audience for the report (and, as it turned out, for the project itself).

Clearly, that project's ethnographic research and writing experience developed in very different ways from the Other Side of Middletown project we have described in several places throughout this book, where community participants were deeply involved in planning the research, interpreting the findings, and shaping the outcome of the final ethnographic manuscript. Though students, faculty, and community members certainly aimed the final ethnographic manuscript at a broad public audience, the local Muncie community was as important an audience as was the more general reader of Middletown history. In many ways, the Middletown project was quite similar to Eric's Kiowa song research (described mostly in the previous chapter), where his Kiowa consultants read and responded to chapters as the ethnography developed (which he then re-integrated back into the text, as in *The Power of Kiowa Song*), or contributed their own written reflections as part of the overall project (as in *The Jesus Road*). Like the Other Side of Middletown project participants, Kiowa consultants appreciated that they were involved in telling an ethnographic story to a larger audience. But they also insisted that the text be readable and relevant to the local audiences who had invested so much of their time and expertise in the manuscript.

Beth's work with museum exhibits on African American pioneers in eastern Indiana (described briefly in chapter 2) moved along a similar trajectory. In that case, the project's textual forms consisted of images, exhibit labels, and compiled sounds rather than reports or manuscripts; the project's intended audience was also much more localized than Eric's Kiowa song research or our Middletown project. The museum for which she produced the exhibit specifically sought to bring local experiences and audiences into their exhibit spaces, so involving the region's African American pioneer descendants in the design, interpretation, and development of the final exhibit was absolutely critical. Although the exhibition's audiences certainly included people in the region who wanted to learn a more complex story about Midwestern agrarianism and the settling of the Old Northwest Territories, the museum's core mission for and, consequently, approach to the exhibit depended on engaging local African Americans in the telling of their own stories.

Beth's Lake County Fair fieldwork (described in chapter 4) moved in a slightly different direction than these other projects. In that case, her work was primarily about preservation; thus, much of that project's audience presumably existed somewhere in the future, in persons who might one day be curious about what Midwestern state fairs used to be like, way back at the beginning of the twenty-first century. (That same – and, we believe, very legitimate – documentary and preservationist impulse is present in many other ethnographic forms as well). Certainly, her immediate audience included the National Endowment for the Humanities, which funded the project, and Traditional Arts Indiana and the Indiana Historical Society, which directed the project and processed, archived, and disseminated its materials. Importantly, the people whom she observed and engaged in conversation were also a primary audience. She regularly shared and discussed her evolving fieldnotes with her interlocutors, using both participant checking and dialogic editing to ensure that no confidential or sensitive information was put on public display, to get a sense of whether or not her observations coincided with those of fair participants, and, importantly, to build the base of trust upon which further conversations would depend. Another project with which Beth was involved more recently developed a website that profiled successful stories of grassroots community development across West Virginia and engaged different sites, circles, and degrees of collaboration. Though, unfortunately, the webpage is no longer available, the project was specifically designed to cultivate working collaborative relationships in the short term, and to support the state's growing grassroots community development network during a time of great transition.

As we have already observed, we have started many projects that, though they may have accomplished other things, never materialized as full or final ethnographic forms. The West Virginia activist oral history project (mentioned in chapter 3) is one example. Similarly, the ethnographic projects we did as students – like Eric's Narcotics Anonymous (NA) ethnography (briefly mentioned in chapter 4) or Beth's ethnographic research with bikers (briefly mentioned in chapter 1) – each deployed varying levels of collaborative engagement. In both Eric's NA research and Beth's bikers' research, consultants read and commented on the ethnographic texts as they developed; processes quite similar to those we deployed in other projects. Still, these were student projects, and they materialized very differently in form. Even though they did, like all of our projects, come to have a life of their own, they were never intended to be full-blown ethnographic projects; they were, after all, conducted in the context of a class or seminar on ethnographic methods. And their audiences were limited to the people with whom we worked, our fellow students, and our professors.

All of this is to say that, just as in fieldwork, engendering ethnographic forms – again, creating the vast range of texts, productions, actions, and new projects that emerge out of ethnography – is a dynamic process very much tied to the particular conditions and relationships around which ethnographic projects are built in the first place. Different ethnographic collaborations materialize in very different ways because they involve different people, organizations, and contexts; these different people, organizations, and contexts, of course, shape every project's end-products in varying ways and with varying levels of power and influence. More than this, the particular ways in which multi-sited collaborations now shape ethnographic fieldwork – which may include a wide range of ideas and assumptions, expectations and hopes, and imaginaries for collaboration (see chapter 2) – also now work to shape final ethnographic forms: this, too, is further changing what "ethnography" is and what it "looks like."

In this chapter, we briefly explore these new ethnographic forms (and the collaborations that engender them), and consider how those forms continue to redefine exactly what ethnography is (i.e., in terms of its various end-products). We follow this with a discussion of how ethnography's new forms – and differently informed approaches to those forms – can work to change ethnography's focus from a kind of research that knows things, to a way of writing that changes things.

EXERCISE – MAKING SENSE OF MATERIALS

When most students first encounter ethnography, it is often through one of two textual forms: in the eminently recognizable literary form discussed early in chapter 1 (examples of which are recommended throughout), or in the equally familiar form of a field, or step-by-step, guide to doing ethnography. From the first, it is possible to glean a sense of place, people, culture, and tradition. The second usually provides some version of "the ethnographic process": develop your research questions, select a site, establish rapport, identify key informants, collect your data, and finally, leave the field (actually or metaphorically) to "write it up." Interestingly, although this last stage certainly depends on writing, the focus of this stage is most often on suggesting hypotheses, recognizing patterns, analyzing data, and developing theory. Some attention is paid to genre and style, of course, but the actual processes of writing are less foregrounded. Writing fades to the background instead, where it remains an almost transparent instrument, albeit – depending on your theoretical orientation or practice – an instrument that should be more representative, or more just, or more aesthetically pleasing than it used to be.

But, as we have tried to emphasize throughout this text, when ethnography's fundamental processes – like fieldwork, conversations, and writing – are humanistically posed and collaboratively enacted, its central emphasis shifts from discovering points of view to constructing understandings and actions. Despite the fact that less attention has been paid to the relationship to the role of inscription – by which we mean putting "words" on "pages" – our contention is that writing has been and remains central to those understandings and actions, and that it underlies ethnography's constitutive and transformative potentials.

As you prepare to inscribe, think about the very substantial collection of "materials" you have at this point. You certainly have ideas, questions, and the beginnings of relationships. You probably have fieldnotes and interview transcripts at this point; you may also have lists of ideas, or outlines of "findings," or bits of rich description. You have probably also produced at least some formative texts.

But now you must turn this jumble of materials into something frighteningly final: a paper, report, or dissertation perhaps, or a presentation, website, film, book, graphic novel, exhibit, or even a plan for action. The shape your ethnographic form eventually takes – whether a traditional manuscript, an action plan, a performance piece, or something else – will depend on what project participants want to emerge out of the work. There may once have been one particular textual form which would have been called "ethnography," but that is not the case anymore. (We will return to this issue in the next Exercise, below.)

One thing that has not changed about ethnography, and which we suspect will never change, is the tremendous challenge that ethnographers face when trying to make sense of their materials. In many ways, deciding to engage people, sites, events, and practices collaboratively makes that already difficult process even more complicated: the cacophony of similarity and difference that resounds throughout any ethnographic enterprise is compounded by the range of opinions, expectations, interpretations, and agendas that are always and everywhere present in collaboration.

But, practically speaking, that does not help very much, does it? The question remains: what to do? How to corral, sort, and make sense of what has emerged in your ethnographic work?

In the more traditionally oriented frames that characterize many field and step-by-step guides, especially those that valorize the scientific method, once the ethnographic data is collected, analytical tools – like domain analysis, event structure analysis, data analysis softwares, and so on – are deployed to suggest and/or test hypotheses, discern patterns, and develop theories, all of which serve an end goal of cultural interpretation and explication.

In keeping with those frames and aims, some ethnographers (and other qualitative researchers) analyze their data utilizing methods like triangulation, a cross-checking process that uses different data points and perspectives to bolster validity and reliability. In some versions of qualitative research, where the research orientation and aims coincide with epistemological concepts like validity and reliability, this makes sense. But when ethnography aims for understanding, action, or transformation, this approach is less appropriate. Going back to the idea of an ethnography that is interpretive and hermeneutic rather than scientistic, we prefer to use terms like "saturation" when describing how this kind of ethnography approaches interpretation. Think about how other humanistic scholars engage their materials, whether ideas, artifacts, texts, expressions, or happenings: they spend time with them, pore over them, read and re-read them, think about them, discuss them with others, write about them, and compare them to other artifacts, texts, expressions, and happenings. Think, too, about how you might engage ethnographic materials in much the same way, and about differences between interpretive processes that are more like immersion, and those that are more like analysis. At some point in that process, intuitions will begin to emerge. Those intuitions – or, more accurately, inklings – will lead to fresh questions, which will lead back into new conversations, on to further questions, and eventually into deeper texts and new understandings (which will lead on to further questions, conversations, and so on).

And now, it is time to begin.

1. Return to the research questions you designed and revised early in the project and read them over. Without referring to notes, take an hour or so to jot down the answers, ideas, situations, and additional questions that come to mind for each.
2. Carve out an extended period of time to immerse yourself in all of the materials you have gathered.[1] Include everything here, from your first positioning statements to your last notes on interview transcripts. (We have listed this carving out of time as a separate exercise because it is essential.)
3. Read all of your materials. Depending on your own goals and preferences, you can do this on your own, with a partner, or with a small group. (We find it helpful to go through all of the materials once on our own, and, ideally, to then go through them again with research collaborators/

community partners after they, too, have gone through the materials on their own.) Study visuals, if you have collected them, and re-listen to sound recordings. Go through everything slowly and thoughtfully, and take notes.

    a. Depending on the size of your project and magnitude of your materials, as a part of your note-taking process you may want to begin indexing (or "coding") your various collected texts. This can be done, simply, as you read, by making lists that reference content where various ideas, concepts, terms, themes, contradictions, and so forth emerge in the texts you are reviewing. (Think of this much like you would think of making an index found in a book, which means, of course, that you will have to create some sort of page numbering system for your materials.) This list will grow, change, and shift as you read, of course, but it will help you find content quickly and make connections between ideas and concepts when you begin writing your final work(s). We should note here, too, that in large projects many ethnographers may choose to use software programs to help them organize materials similarly. (Information about programs like ATLAS-ti, Ethnograph, or NVivo are readily available online). Such software can be enormously helpful, and can be used in ways that do not necessarily compromise the textual processes of hermeneutics and interpretation.[2] It can be tempting, though, to use such software to organize materials and output codes without having to engage in "deep reading" of the texts themselves. Think of it this way: you can quickly access information and learn a lot about a book from its index; but you will potentially miss quite a bit if you do not actually *read* the book.

    b. After reading through all of your materials, return to your research questions and summarize them again. How is the response you wrote in the first part of this Exercise different from the one you are writing now? Do the answers you are coming up with make sense to you (and to the others with whom you are working)? Are there any surprises? Are there questions you do not have answers to? Questions you would ask now that you could not have thought of before?

4. Begin to write more extensive responses to the research questions, being sure to cite the interviews, conversations, observations, fieldnotes, and so on which inform your developing ideas.

5. Continue to read and write, and focus your conversations on insights and ideas as they emerge. Keep sharing your texts, and keep incorporating the

group's changing ideas back into the evolving text. (We will have more to say about this process in the next Exercise.)

Be advised that this is a long, slow, and sometimes arduous process, and that the tentative – and sometimes tenuous – nature of this process can be disconcerting, especially for those who are new to it. But this discomfort is both the very nature of emergence – which, again, asks for more than spontaneous follow-up questions – and the place from which ethnography's unanticipated outcomes often arise.

"What is Ethnography?" Redux: On the Emergence of Contemporary Ethnographic Forms

As we noted in chapter 1, many view ethnography as both a fieldwork method and an approach to writing. As such, "ethnography" can refer to the genre's particular literary tradition, traditionally book-length manuscripts that exhibit certain characteristics that make them "ethnographic" in form and thus different from other literary genres (like novels or biographies). Part of what makes these works distinctive (and distinctively ethnographic) is a focus on documenting fieldwork (which incorporates, to varying degrees, elements of participation, observation, and dialogue within the text); a concerted effort to explore meaningful systems of behavior and experience (which some might call "culture"); an emphasis on how actors negotiate as well as navigate such systems from an experiential point of view (what some refer to, in Malinowskian terms, as "the native point of view"); and – perhaps above all – an engagement with a particular kind of storytelling informed by ethnographic theory and method (which is always ongoing and emergent, of course).

Ethnographic texts across time and space also share a distinct style: they dwell within a specific literary tradition, foreground fieldwork, explore systems of meaning from an experiential point of view, and tell a particular kind of story. As anthropologist Paul Stoller observes, beyond imparting a "sense of locality" (i.e., of place) and depicting believable "construction[s] of character" (i.e., of the people who live or work within that particular place), the best ethnographies also manage to tell compelling human stories:

> Even if you sensuously describe the physical attributes of the ethnographic locale and sensitively construct the character of the people who live there, you have only met the necessary, but not the sufficient conditions of memorable ethnography. For the latter, ethnographers as well as their characters need to grapple with the things that are most fundamentally human – love and loss, fear and courage, fate and compassion – deep

issues that connect readers to the people they encounter in ethnographic texts. "Yes," you might say, "I can identify with the author and the friends he describes."[3]

Not all ethnographic texts achieve the status of "memorable ethnography," but we think this is a good endpoint for which to aim – and also a good beginning point to start our discussion of forms and possibilities for ethnographic texts, wherever the place, whoever the characters, and whatever the project.

*****

What is considered "an ethnography" has changed several times throughout the genre's history. As we have noted earlier, many ethnographic descriptions of the late nineteenth and early twentieth century – now often thought of as salvage ethnography – concentrated on documenting what were then perceived to be dying or disappearing indigenous cultures. Because many of these early ethnographers also saw their work as interventions into the hegemony of European history that could add to and complicate the larger story of human experience, they took pains to include minutely detailed descriptions of stories, legends, mythologies, and other cultural narratives in their ethnographic manuscripts, often with little to no commentary on the part of the ethnographer.[4]

These more historically focused ethnographies began to give way to new ethnographic forms as social scientists turned away from elaborating cultural histories and toward more generally explaining the functions of human behavior. Malinowski's pioneering ethnographic work, in particular, marked a major transition, not only in how ethnographers would approach fieldwork (which we discussed briefly in chapter 4), but in how ethnographers would write ethnographic texts. Though similar in some ways to earlier salvage ethnographies, which also focused on native experiences and perspectives, this new form of ethnography highlighted how different parts of a cultural system (e.g., those political, economic, or religious) functioned together, holistically, to form "culture" and, in turn, *in*form people's behavior. In the original 500-page-plus *Argonauts of the Western Pacific*, for example, Malinowski presents readers with numerous and various discussions of tribal history and mythology; magic and other local belief systems; work and leisure activities; the building, launching, and sailing of canoes; tribal economics and the sociology of trade – just to name a few – all of which point to the final chapter, "The Meaning of the Kula." That chapter, as the title suggests, seeks to explain the underlying function and meaning of the Kula, a major Trobriand cultural institution and the topic of Malinowski's study, which connected a broad constellation of socio-religious, economic, and political practices via the exchange of arm shells and shell necklaces throughout the Trobriand islands.[5]

Theorizing and explaining how culture functioned as a system was a significant turning point in the "look" and "feel" of ethnographic texts. So, too, was the heightened focus on participation and observation, which, as we discussed earlier, also lent an air of scientific authority to ethnographic explanations like Malinowski's.[6] Powerful schools of thought in anthropology and sociology (such as at Columbia University or the University of Chicago) then ensconced the writing of ethnography within a decidedly scientific, comparativist stance, and by mid-century it was not uncommon for ethnographic texts to engage larger theories of behavior, culture, or psychology. It was into this context that many ethnographers – beginning in the 1960s and 1970s – launched well-known critiques of the limitations of these scientistically oriented ethnographic forms. Perhaps the most well-known of these were the writings of anthropologist Clifford Geertz, who, in publications like *The Interpretation of Cultures*, famously (and almost single-handedly) shifted ethnography's orientation from one focused on positivism and deduction to one focused on interpretation and meaning. Doing ethnography, Geertz suggested, should involve us not in the reduction of human activity and meaning to simple universalizing models; it should instead involve us in the more complex, nuanced, and intellectual traditions of reading and analyzing texts. Doing and writing (as well as reading) ethnography, Geertz thus argued, ultimately involved ethnographers in textual processes of elucidating meaning via "thick description" of ethnographic subjects and topics. "The culture of a people," Geertz famously wrote, "is an ensemble of texts, themselves ensembles, which the anthropologist strains to read over the shoulders of those to whom they properly belong."[7]

Geertz's critiques, along with others, helped to re-establish ethnography as primarily an interpretive affair (as we briefly discussed in the Introduction), which, along with accompanying moves of symbolic and interpretivist anthropologists that followed, shifted the "look" and "feel" of ethnographic texts yet again.[8] The couching of ethnography within the interpretive social sciences and humanities – as well as the critiques of prior forms that accompanied that shift – opened the field to a wide range of experimental ethnographies, in which ethnographers experimented with textual forms by employing literary devices like narrative, memoir, dialogue, poetry, and even fiction to convey experience cross-culturally. (Tedlock's narrative ethnography, discussed in chapter 4, is a good example of this kind of experiment). Such experiments blurred the boundaries between ethnography and other literary genres, of course. But importantly, these experiments (some of which took inspiration from a similar movement in the 1920s and 1930s inspired by the likes of Zora Neale Hurston and Elsie Clews Parsons) also provided further context for interrogating previous assumptions attached to ethnography and for reconceptualizing its doing and writing in ways more attuned to the complexities of the late twentieth century.[9]

In the 1970s, 1980s, and 1990s, feminists, postmodernists, and other critical theorists fundamentally interrogated the patriarchal and colonial history underlying ethnography's emergence and ongoing practice – regularly reified in ethnographic texts of all stripes – and suggested a broad range of alternatives for "de-colonizing" ethnography.[10] Feminists, for instance, levied serious critiques at the androcentricity behind much ethnography, in which male ethnographers, often working only with other men in the field, extrapolated their findings to represent entire communities, in effect deploying accepted rhetorical strategies for ethnographic inscription that, quite literally, "wrote off" half of a population.[11] Feminist ethnography thus often problematized the forms of ethnographic work as well as the processes of fieldwork itself, focusing on how knowledge is positioned within systems of inequity (gender, of course, being primary among these). In an effort to de-colonize and democratize the processes of ethnographic fieldwork and writing, feminist ethnographers extended issues of positionality into their ethnographic writing experiments, using devices like biography, dialogic editing, or reciprocal ethnography, a kind of collaborative ethnography informed by feminist theory in which ethnographers share their ethnographic texts with and seek input from their consultants as the writing develops.[12] For example, in her reciprocal ethnography, *Holy Women, Wholly Women*, folklorist Elaine Lawless described the process as "feminist because it insists on a denial of hierarchical constructs that place the scholar at some apex of knowledge and understanding and her 'subjects' in some inferior, less knowledgeable position. This approach seeks to privilege no voice over another and relies on dialogue as the key to understanding and illumination."[13]

In many ways, these feminist ethnographies were similar to what has been called postmodern ethnography, ethnographic texts that also explicitly problematized issues of voice and representation, power, and authority. Though most so-called postmodernist theorists eschewed the term "postmodern" to describe their works, they nonetheless questioned the many and varied assumptions that framed ethnographic fieldwork and writing during its formative, modernist development in the early and mid-twentieth century – including its more recent manifestations within interpretive frameworks as put forward by those like Geertz. A well-known and still oft-cited collection of essays, *Writing Culture: The Poetics and Politics of Ethnography*, published in 1986, captured the spirit of that time. In the book's Introduction, James Clifford noted that the book's authors:

> see culture as composed of seriously contested codes and representations; they assume that the poetic and the political are inseparable, that science is in, not above, historical and linguistic processes. They assume that academic and literary genres interpenetrate and that the writing of cultural descriptions is properly experimental and ethical. Their focus on text making and rhetoric serves to highlight the constructed, artificial nature of cultural accounts. It undermines overly transparent modes of authority, and it draws attention to the historical predicament of ethnography, the fact that it is always caught up in the invention, not the representation, of cultures....[14]

Ethnography, in this view, is always partial, tentative, and emergent; never innocently produced; and always rhetorical: even ostensibly corrective literary devices like "thick description" (that Geertz advocated), some argued, merely reinforced the authority and power of the ethnographer to speak for others while at the same time veiling the actual dialogic processes at work behind collaboratively based understandings. An overarching message in these critiques was that it did not have to be this way: attention to ethnographic inscription called for experiments in and with ethnographic writing, which had great potential to transform ethnography itself. Importantly, the aim of these interrogations was not to produce a more accurate or "true" ethnography; instead, ethnography's "experimental moment" sought different goals for ethnography and different kinds of ethnographic practice. Clifford, for example, pointed out that "the principle of dialogical textual production goes well beyond the more or less artful presentation of 'actual' encounters. It locates cultural interpretations in many sorts of reciprocal contexts, and it obliges writers to find diverse ways of rendering negotiated realities as multisubjective, power-laden, and incongruent."[15]

Many ethnographers had been writing various kinds of dialogic ethnography by this time – a kind of ethnographic writing that foregrounds field conversations so as to evoke intersubjective and cross-cultural understandings of experience.[16] Such ethnographies helped to de-center ethnographic authority and highlight reciprocal contexts for knowledge production in ways much like reflexive ethnography or autoethnography, first-person ethnographic writing styles that, somewhat like narrative ethnography, highlight the experience of ethnographers via literary devices like autobiography or personal narrative. "A reflexive ethnography is like travel in one's own country," wrote anthropologist Dan Rose in a well-known book of the time, *Black American Street Life*, "in that the anthropologist – or cultural journalist, for that matter – looks to other humans as varieties of the *self* rather than as varieties of the *other*."[17] While some of these reflexive texts were criticized for being self-indulgent, textual forms like autoethnography achieve great potential, suggests sociologist and communication studies scholar Carolyn Ellis, when conceived as "research, writing, story, and method that connect the autobiographical and personal to the cultural, social, and political."[18]

All of these various and diverse impulses for doing and writing ethnography, from feminist to postmodernist, from dialogic to autoethnographic, helped to give rise to new forms of what were being called critical ethnographies, which, while often stressing critiques of taken-for-granted social, cultural, political, or economic institutions, also emphasized the ethical, dialogic, and political underpinnings of – and potentials for – ethnography in very open and self-conscious ways.[19] In this sense, new critical understandings of how ethnography worked could be mobilized for social change. "Conventional ethnographers study culture for the purpose of describing it," wrote sociologist Jim Thomas in his book titled *Doing Critical Ethnography*; "critical ethnographers do so to change it. Conventional ethnographers recognize the impossibility, and the undesirability, of research that is free of normative and other biases, but believe that these biases are to be repressed. Critical ethnographers instead celebrate their normative and political position as a means of invoking social consciousness and societal change."[20]

These newer critical ethnographies have genealogies that extend back to earlier works like Margaret Mead's 1928 *Coming of Age in Samoa*, in which Mead used her study of Samoan adolescence as the basis for a comparative commentary on American adolescence that offered possibilities for action. If culture is learned, Mead argued in *Coming of Age*, Americans can learn from alternative ways of being and acting – in this case, of Samoans – to change aspects of their own societies with which they are dissatisfied.[21] Unlike those of the past, however, these new critical and self-conscious approaches for doing and writing ethnography slowly moved from the margins of ethnographic theory and practice to the center. And by the beginning of the twenty-first century, ethnography had also moved a bit closer to other forms of applied, participatory, and action research.[22] Different approaches and forms of applied ethnography expanded into even broader realms of activity that used ethnographic field methods and approaches to address local issues and problems.[23] Various kinds of collaborative research, like collaborative ethnography – in which ethnographers and their consultants work together, in different ways and to varying degrees, to design, implement, and even write ethnography collaboratively – took on a renewed energy and vibrancy. So, too, did the various kinds of collaborative and participatory action research that could emanate from such projects.[24]

Integrations of collaborative research activity, ethnographic writing, and activism have happened before – applied and action researches, in fact, reach back decades.[25] But today these active and activist tendencies intersect within contemporary contexts for doing and writing ethnography, in particular, in more direct and pronounced ways. For one, they now surface into streams of ethnographic praxis where clear divisions between fieldwork and ethnographic texts have collapsed – as have hard-and-fast separations between data and interpretation, theory and practice, "pure research" and application.[26] Also, because they now often materialize within new tropes of and imaginaries for collaboration (as we discussed in chapter 2), the mixing of various elements of collaboration, research, writing, and action have led to an even broader array of possible ethnographic forms. The projects we mention in the opening of this chapter have engendered other ethnographically inspired products beyond those already mentioned, products like documentary videos and photographs, websites, interpretive exhibitions, ethnographic song recordings, articles and essays, papers and presentations to colleagues and community groups.[27] These projects have also called up a wide range of collaborative actions and activisms – all of which, as we noted above, have emerged in very particular ways that are often very specific to the contexts of their original collaborations. Although ethnographic films, song recordings, exhibitions, and presentations – and even activisms with or on behalf of ethnographic collaborators – have emerged out of ethnography for a very long time, the range of collaboratively inspired work that now inhabits the term "ethnographic" has expanded exponentially.

EXERCISE – WRITING ETHNOGRAPHY

Although ethnographers may express loosely agreed-upon notions of what makes a text "ethnographic" (such as seen in Stoller's comments above), the many different forms of ethnography now available make it abundantly clear that there is no single form or one way to write ethnography today. Moreover, and as we have repeatedly emphasized, each ethnographic project is different, and differently organized around unique sets of relationships and collaborations. As such, each textual form that emerges out of every particular ethnographic enterprise will be very much project-bound and deeply contextual. Making decisions about what and how to write a final ethnographic piece (whether book, report, paper, or website), then, can be challenging; but it can also be incredibly rewarding because it encourages us to look to conversation and dialogue about the evolving ethnography itself to make decisions about how our final text will materialize.

Take another extended example from the Other Side of Middletown project. As per the discussions with Goodall (as described earlier in chapter 2), we knew at the outset that we wanted to write a book. That provided us the framework for "imagining" what our final ethnography would look like; but that, of course, could take many different forms. Only through further discussion did we eventually decide to organize the book into two parts. Faculty and community experts would write the first part on the history of Muncie's African American community as well as Middletown as a research site, both of which would help provide important historic and social context for the book's second, and much longer, part. Students in collaboration with teams of community members would write Part II. We organized each team around a chapter heading. Importantly, the chapter headings in Part II followed those in the original 1929 *Middletown* study (for example, "Getting a Living," "Making a Home," "Training the Young," etc.), which provided the "umbrella" area of study on which the teams would focus both their fieldwork and their writing (the "Getting a Living" team, for example, would focus their study on things like work and small black businesses).

The similarities between the classic study and our ethnography ended there, however. In consultation with the larger collaborative research team, students and community members chose and negotiated research questions, decided on fieldwork trajectories (including which events to attend or who to interview), collected archival materials, and read relevant literature (such as the original *Middletown*, and other works on Muncie's black community). Each team organized their developing materials (particularly fieldnotes, interview logs/transcripts, and developing indexes) as portfolios; portfolios that were kept in a central location to be used for cross-referencing when students began to write their chapters. The Introduction to *The Other Side of Middletown* includes an extensive discussion of this writing process, so we will not describe it in detail here.[28] In sum: though that process was lengthy and time-consuming, shifting and changing as we went, we made several decisions about what the chapters themselves would "look" and "feel" like before and during the writing process. To augment the sense of locality, we agreed that each chapter should include edited excerpts from fieldnotes (in many cases fieldnote descriptions were integrated directly into the text to provide context, for example). To couch the work in experience and the collaborative process, we agreed that every chapter should include discussion of personal experience and how the relationship between community advisors and students specifically influenced the direction of any given team's fieldwork (in most cases, we agreed that these should come at the beginning or end of the chapter). To more closely elaborate content and intent of certain kinds of speech (preaching, for example), we agreed to use poetic transcription where appropriate.[29] To connect with larger literatures and discussions about Middletown and Muncie's African American community (as was elaborated in the book's first part), we agreed to pull from archival sources, from the community literature we had collected, and from the original *Middletown*. Along these lines, we decided on an overall style and approach that would mix narrative with scholarly approach (and agreed we would cite all sources – literature, interviews, community consultation, for example – using an endnote style per the *Chicago Manual of Style*). And, perhaps most importantly, to animate the text with voices from the Muncie community, we agreed that dialogue and conversation would, to the best of our abilities as writers, serve as the base and framework for each chapter's discussion: dialogue would ideally "drive" points made, not just embellish them (such as, in the latter case, when a quote is used to illustrate a point made by an author). What this meant, of course, was that the "stories" of fieldnotes and field interviews and conversations were centralized in the writing process, and they served as the base around which our ethnography was ultimately built. But that was just the beginning. As the chapter drafts developed, these were shared with community advisors and consultants, interviewees, faculty, and the larger research team in both private and public forums; responses to the texts were then integrated back into the text as this dialogic reviewing process began anew.

The particular writing process we have just described represents a very specific case, where the goals, agendas, and imaginings of a very particular group involved in a very particular set of conversations led to a very particular ethnographic form (with all the limitations and possibilities that implies). Although we realize, again, that there is no one single form or way to write ethnography, in this Exercise, we ask that you consider what your "final" ethnographic product might "look" like. (Of course, your facilitator or instructor, too, may have certain expectations of what your final ethnographic text should be). With this in mind, consider the following, and in dialogue with your research partners, consultants, or other ethnographic collaborators, consider:

1. What are the text's ultimate goals? To describe or inform? To fill in a historical void? To compel some kind of change or action?
2. What kind of ethnographic text will you produce? What form will it take? For example: are you producing a short paper, community website, poster, conference paper, book, report, video, or audio broadcast?
3. How will you organize your text? As chapters, as in a book? As sections, as in a class paper? As different pages, as in a website or blog? As interpretive texts or labels, as in exhibit panels or in posters? In scenes or vignettes, as in a video or audio production?
4. How will you incorporate individual voices? Will every chapter or section, for example, begin with an individual's story? How will you give a sense of locality? How will you include descriptions of places, events, or gatherings? How often will you do this?
5. What style or voice will your project take? Will it "sound" like a scholarly report? A narrative? Will it be presented as a collage of first-person person stories? Will you use unified, fragmented, or juxtaposed narratives? Will you experiment with literary devices like allegory, for example, or paradox?
6. How will you represent experience, both your own and that of your collaborators?

7. How will you integrate dialogue (from interviews and conversations, for example)?
8. What other literature will you cite? How will these sources bear on your discussion? In what ways will you bring your work into conversation with those other texts?

Use these discussions as a basis to frame the text you and your collaborators imagine your ethnographic text taking.

Toward Collaborative Writing and Transformation

Despite this very broad range of contemporary ethnographic forms, our essential position is that constructing ethnographic texts remains an integral – albeit an ever-shifting – part of doing ethnography. As in the past, the "look" and "feel" of those texts continues to change along with their aims and orientations; although singling out (or deploying) all the different styles and kinds of experimental ethnography does not currently seem to carry the significance it did a generation ago, ethnography has been forever changed by these developments. Indeed, it is now next to impossible for ethnographers to ignore issues of positionality, voice and representation, power and authority (inherited from feminist and postmodern ethnography); relationships between Self and Other (inherited from reflexive ethnography); the importance of literary devices like (auto)biography and story (inherited from the likes of auto- and narrative ethnography); how dialogic understandings develop in the process of creating ethnography (inherited from dialogic ethnography) and their potential for co-authorship and co-production (inherited from the likes of reciprocal and collaborative ethnography); and importantly, the now intrinsic roles of action and application in ethnographic praxis (inherited from applied and critical ethnography).

Interestingly, alongside these theoretical developments – and despite the textual emphases within which so many of those developments were embedded – the activist potentials of ethnographic *writing* have been largely eschewed. Ethnography's possibilities for action have been and remain couched within more conventionally critical or demonstrative forms of field- or policy-based action and activism. Continued and deeply held assumptions about ethnographic writing that cast it as an artifact, a tool in the ethnographer's kit, or even as a literary experiment, have very effectively masked what we (particularly Beth) have elsewhere called writing's constitutive potential, wherein the processes, products, and acts of *writing together* change what people know about each other, how they are with each other, and, eventually, who individual participants are.[30]

Over recent decades, literacy scholars have begun to embrace an idea of writing as "*social, ideological,* and *constitutive.*"[31] In light of our Middletown experience – and many of our other ethnographic experiences as well – the idea of writing as constitutive, where, as literacy scholar Marilyn Cooper put it, "people relate as complete, social beings, rather than imagining each other as remote images" is especially compelling.[32] What is interesting about that idea, and where it connects to ethnography and ethnographic writing, is the way in which it reorients thinking about writing in terms of what writing can *do,* rather than how it is made or what it communicates.

In some ways, ethnographic writing's constitutive potential could easily have emerged from the very developments that disregarded that possibility. After all, most of ethnography's theoretical developments – from the earliest historical interventions into European hegemony to its more recent iterations in feminist theory, participatory action, activism, and so on – proceed from the idea and the desire that ethnographic work can and should contribute to social change. (This is true in the case of ethnography's darker manifestations as well.) But even though ethnographers have fundamentally interrogated and reformulated many of ethnography's elements in ways that illuminate constitutive potentialities, ethnographic writing has yet to receive that same attention.

It is understandable, but that understanding took years to become apparent to us. We had certainly noted the interesting relationships that rose out of producing and sharing written texts, although it was not until the Other Side of Middletown project that we really began to understand the constitutive powers of ethnographic writing that works between people. Beth, who served as the project's editor, has written about how that understanding began to emerge:

> I found myself in the position of having to pay a great deal of attention to what *writing* our ethnography was *doing.* I had known for some time that fieldwork formed and often deepened relationships between people. But as we all wrote together in *Middletown,* trading the developing texts constantly back and forth between us, I began to see that it wasn't just being together "in the field" that led to new ways of thinking about and being with each other. In Middletown, the processes, products, and acts of *writing together* – of crafting, navigating, and negotiating the clumps of words that would eventually form our ethnographic text – were forming and transforming the relationships between us.[33]

As we noted in chapter 4, the idea of ethnographic writing with which we are working is a kind of "writing with," where ethnographers produce, share, and negotiate texts with or alongside participants.[34] Issues of power and voice, of who speaks, and of who speaks for whom, call for collaborative approaches that ask us to write *with* rather than *about* others and to be aware of our *selves* in the world. Again, collaborative writing approaches can strengthen our connections to, rather than our distances from, the people with whom we work and about whom we write. As with every other aspect of ethnographic work, how the details of these processes work out differs widely from project to project. At the heart of this "writing together," there is a focus on relationships and collaborative processes, where the writing is an actor rather than a tool. Writing then does much more than merely record what happens: it becomes the site, the medium, and the activity within which those "happenings" occur.[35]

In collaborative contexts, ethnographic writing does much more than communicate or represent; it works between people, *making* and *remaking* the individuals, communities, and issues it engages. And, as with other collaborative practice, it does so from positions of generosity and faithfulness: a generosity that asks participants to approach others from positions of openness, compassion, and respect, and a faithfulness that asks participants to honor the project's shared commitments. These are *ways of being* characterized by honesty, seriousness, respect, and vulnerability, and they are grounded in the idea that we all have as much to learn from each other, as we have to teach each other. The idea is not that collaboratively enacted ethnographic writing leads to some kind of a blind and perfect communion, but that it offers something beyond knowledge for its own sake.[36]

In many ways, since ethnographic forms first appeared more than a century ago, they have been moving – inexorably, we would argue – toward the idea that ethnography can work between people to craft understanding. Clearly, we see great promise in ethnographic writing's constitutive power, where the focus is not on what writing discovers or argues or represents, but rather on what it *makes of writers in the writing*. In the constitutive and relational natures of writing and ethnography – and the near limitless potentialities of both – we see opportunities to *literally* write different ways of being.[37]

EXERCISE – COLLABORATIVE WRITING

Just as interpretation was once posed in relatively linear and uncritical terms – moving from research questions to rapport to data to interpretation to publication – writing was often posed as a process that ran in a straight line from prewriting, through drafting, and on to revising and editing. But for decades now, literacy scholars have been working with the understanding that writing is a fundamentally recursive process, and that writers constantly cycle through – or bounce between – these different phases.[38] Literacy scholars have also been working to discredit two assumptions about writing that remain, too often, uninterrogated:

- The first assumption is that writing is some kind of a neutral or transparent tool. As we hope we have made clear, it most certainly is not. Writing does much more than record or present ideas. Both the processes and the products of writing shape thought, form opinions, change minds, inspire commitments, and compel actions. (And more.)
- The second assumption is that authorship is, somehow, the product of an individual mind. (Two images come to mind: the first is a wan novelist who pines away in a dusty garret; the second is an anthropologist or folklorist in the field hunched over his notebook and furiously scribbling away.) This second assumption (or better, ideal) has maintained surprising currency, despite its thorough and ongoing deconstruction in scholarly circles which still – and simultaneously – continue to valorize the single-author manuscript and its accompanying ideas of individual inspiration and genius. (And while we are at it, we guarantee that the ideas expressed in this paragraph will inspire another especially interesting and memorable class or group discussion.)

We think it important to point out these still powerful ideas because the very idea of collaborative writing is fundamentally at odds with them. In contemporary ethnography, the interwoven field, dialogic, interpretive, and writing processes work – emergently, recursively, and constitutively – to raise, share, process, revisit, and re-create a project's emergent conversations, experiences, actions, understandings, and relationships.

Once you have begun to wrestle with these very complex notions of writing and have committed yourselves to writing in ways that embrace that complexity, you will need to negotiate what writing will look like and how it will work with and within your own project. You will also need to become willing to produce and share texts that are still evolving. For a host of reasons that have to do with authority, professionalism, and vulnerability, that is actually much harder to do than it seems. Interestingly, though, we have discovered that producing and sharing partial or unfinished texts is another way to more fully engage participants and extend collaborative practice. The absences in our unfinished texts, the holes, the mistakes, and the half-formed ideas, become a kind of welcome that invites in the people with whom we work.

Throughout these exercises, we have repeatedly turned back to collaborative processes that involve writing (and re-writing), discussing (and re-discussing), and making (and re-making) decisions. We have also emphasized, repeatedly, how the myriad contexts within which projects emerge make each project very specific and particular. Indeed, different ethnographers have written about the different ways in which they have gone about writing their collaborative ethnographies. Eric details several of these in his book, *The Chicago Guide to Collaborative Ethnography*, and they can include processes such as "using principal consultants as readers and editors; employing focus groups, editorial boards, collaborative ethnographer/consultant teams, and community forums; and creating co-written texts."[39]

At this point, though, you have probably already begun to work out a collaborative writing process for your particular context and project (especially because previous exercises have already pushed you in this direction). In some cases, some group members might produce rough drafts while the rest read and comment on those drafts; in others, all of those involved might produce bits of text and work collaboratively to weave them together; in still other projects, different group members might take full responsibility for different sections or aspects of the overall text.

Whatever the form your particular collaboration takes, cooperation and transparency will be critical to its success. In the case of collaborative writing, that is especially true. Those involved in the writing processes must find effective ways to produce and share their own ideas and interpretations, remain open to the ideas and interpretations of others, and be willing to negotiate how those agreements and disagreements will appear "on the page."

For this final Exercise, we suggest a discussion (or series of discussions) that focuses on exploring the particulars of your own project's writing processes thus far, as a way of both examining the shape your own experience took and reflecting on the experiences of others.

1. On your own, spend some time writing about your experience. You can use the questions below as a guide, but feel free to address others.
   a. Describe, from your own point of view, how your text was written. How, specifically, did the process work? How were responsibilities distributed? How were those responsibilities negotiated?
   b. Describe the particular writing processes – both individual and collective – that seemed to work best for you, personally. What aspects were especially easy or comfortable for you? What aspects were difficult or uncomfortable?
   c. Describe how you (and your group) decided what would ultimately appear "on the (final) page." What values, commitments, or events guided those decisions?
   d. Think about a particular time when the writing process worked well, and describe it. Why do you think it went well?

2. Think openly, and with others, about a particular time when things did not go well, and describe that. What do you think happened? Come together with your project partners for a larger discussion around the following:
   a. Share your answers to the questions you have explored on your own.
   b. Where do your experiences and interpretations coincide and differ?
   c. What surprises you most about those coincidences and differences?
3. In your large group (and it is up to you, of course, who to include here), engage in a final discussion around these suggested issues:
   a. How has your project benefitted from this kind of an approach? Which benefits, in particular, did you *not* anticipate?
   b. How has this approach limited your project's possibilities?
   c. What would you do differently next time?
   d. What would you say to others who are about to begin their own collaborative projects?

Suggested Readings

Behar, Ruth, and Deborah A. Gordon, eds. 1995. *Women Writing Culture*. Berkeley: University of California Press. An important, and now classic, collection of essays that explore the poetics and politics of ethnography from a variety of feminist perspectives. We recommend that it be read alongside other critical texts from so-called postmodernist theory, such as *Writing Culture*, included in this list, below.

Clair, Robin Patric, ed. 2003. *Expressions of Ethnography: Novel Approaches to Qualitative Methods*. Albany: State University of New York Press. An eclectic collection of essays largely from communication studies on doing and writing ethnography. The authors draw from a broad range of perspectives, approaches, literary devices, and genres.

Clifford, James, and George E. Marcus, eds. 2010. *Writing Culture: The Poetics and Politics of Ethnography*, 2nd ed. Berkeley: University of California Press. Originally published in 1986, this collection of essays is perhaps the most well-known – and controversial – of texts on writing new forms of ethnography post Geertz. The second edition includes a new Foreword, which, in part, traces impacts and responses since its original publication. We recommend that it be read alongside other critical texts from feminist theory, such as *Women Writing Culture*, included in this list, above.

Denzin, Norman K., and Yvonna S. Lincoln. 2013. *Collecting and Interpreting Qualitative Materials*, 4th ed. London: Sage. This collection includes a broad range of techniques and approaches from several different disciplines for interpreting qualitatively researched material.

Lassiter, Luke Eric. 2005. *The Chicago Guide to Collaborative Ethnography*. Chicago: University of Chicago Press. This book includes a survey of many of the developments behind contemporary collaborative approaches to ethnography (Part I), as well as highlighting how different ethnographers go about doing and writing collaborative ethnography (Part II).

Suggested Websites

The Neighborhood Story Project – www.neighborhoodstoryproject.org/ An exemplary community development program based in New Orleans that uses collaborative ethnography and other methods to co-create a variety of community-based, collaboratively researched, written, and produced books and other media.

Oral History in the Digital Age – http://ohda.matrix.msu.edu/ An extensive site connecting users to a broad range of information about linking digital technologies and media with doing, preserving, and disseminating oral history and other ethnographic work today.

Notes

1. In our current positions, we work primarily with graduate students who are also working professionals – and parents, and children, and siblings, and active members of their communities – and we do know how difficult it is to carve out these unadulterated chunks of time. But we must insist that you find some way to do this, especially when you are going through the entire mass of materials you have gathered for the first time.
2. See, for example, Manfred Max Bergman, "Hermeneutic Content Analysis: Textual and Audiovisual Analyses within a Mixed Method Framework," in *SAGE Handbook of Mixed Methods in Social & Behavioral Research*, 2nd ed., edited by Abbas Tashakkori and Charles Teddlie (London: Sage, 2010), 379–396.
3. Paul Stoller, *The Power of the Between: An Anthropological Odyssey* (Chicago: University of Chicago Press, 2009).
4. See, for example, Paul Radin, *The Method and Theory of Ethnology: An Essay in Criticism* (New York: McGraw-Hill, 1933). See also Regna Darnell, *Invisible Genealogies: A History of Americanist Anthropology* (Lincoln: University of Nebraska Press, 2001); and, *And Along Came Boas: Continuity and Revolution in Americanist Anthropology* (Amsterdam: John Benjamins, 1998).
5. See Bronislaw Malinowski, *Argonauts of the Western Pacific* (London: Routledge, 1922).
6. See James Clifford, "On Ethnographic Authority," *Representations* 1 (1983): 118–146.
7. Clifford Geertz, *The Interpretation of Cultures* (New York: Basic Books, 1973), 452.
8. See George E. Marcus and Michael M. J. Fischer, *Anthropology as Cultural Critique: An Experimental Moment in the Human Sciences* (Chicago: University of Chicago Press, 1986), 17–44.
9. Marcus and Fischer, *Anthropology as Cultural Critique*, 45–76.

10. For more on this, see Luke Eric Lassiter, *The Chicago Guide to Collaborative Ethnography* (Chicago: University of Chicago Press, 2005), 48–75.

11. See, for example, Michelle Rosaldo and Louise Lamphere, eds., *Women, Culture, and Society* (Stanford, CA: Stanford University Press, 1974).

12. See, for example, Elaine Lawless, *Holy Women, Wholly Women: Sharing Ministries through Life Stories and Reciprocal Ethnography* (Philadelphia: University of Pennsylvania Press, 1993).

13. Lawless, *Holy Women, Wholly Women*, 5.

14. James Clifford and George Marcus, eds., *Writing Culture: The Poetics and Politics of Ethnography* (Berkeley: University of California Press, 1986), 2.

15. Clifford and Marcus, eds., *Writing Culture*, 15.

16. See, for example, Kevin Dwyer, *Moroccan Dialogues: Anthropology in Question* (Baltimore, MD: The Johns Hopkins University Press, 1982).

17. Dan Rose, *Black American Street Life: South Philadelphia, 1969–1971* (Philadelphia: University of Pennsylvania Press, 1987), 4.

18. Carolyn Ellis, *The Ethnographic I: A Methodological Novel about Autoethnography* (Walnut Creek, CA: AltaMira Press, 2004), xix.

19. See Marcus and Fischer, *Anthropology as Cultural Critique*, 77–164.

20. Jim Thomas, *Doing Critical Ethnography* (London: Sage, 1993), 4.

21. See Marcus and Fischer, *Anthropology as Cultural Critique*, 111–164.

22. See George Marcus, ed., *Critical Ethnography Now: Unexpected Contexts, Shifting Constituencies, Changing Agendas* (Santa Fe, NM: School of American Research Press, 1999).

23. See, for example, Erve Chambers, "Applied Ethnography," in *Collecting and Interpreting Qualitative Materials*, eds. Norman K. Denzin and Yvonna S. Lincoln (London: Sage, 2003), 389–418.

24. For more on this, see Lassiter, *Chicago Guide to Collaborative Ethnography*, 48ff.

25. See Peter Reason and Hilary Bradbury, eds., *The Sage Handbook of Action Research: Participatory Inquiry and Practice*, 2nd ed. (London: Sage, 2008).

26. For a fuller discussion of these trends within the field of anthropology, for instance, see Les W. Field and Richard G. Fox, eds., *Anthropology Put to Work* (Oxford: Berg, 2007).

27. For example: a documentary video (*Middletown Redux*, available from AltaMira Press) and photo exhibit ("The Other Side of Middletown," at the Indiana State Museum in 2007) accompanied the Other Side of Middletown project; various websites accompanied that project and have accompanied many of Beth's museum exhibits, such as for the African American pioneers exhibit mentioned in the main text of this chapter's introduction; several professionally produced ethnographic song recordings grew out of Eric's work with Kiowas; and, of course, a great many papers and presentations to colleagues and community groups have materialized from all of our projects.

28. See Luke Eric Lassiter, Hurley Goodall, Elizabeth Campbell, Michelle Natasya Johnson, eds., *The Other Side of Middletown: Exploring Muncie's African American Community* (Walnut Creek, CA: AltaMira Press, 2004), esp. 16–22. The documentary, *Middletown Redux* (Walnut Creek, CA: AltaMira Press, 2004), also includes a section on the writing process and the particular way in which the ethnography was written between and among students and their community partners.

29. For more on this, see Lassiter et al., *The Other Side of Middletown*, 17. For more on poetic transcription (also called "ethnopoetics"), see, for example, Dennis Tedlock, *The Spoken Word and Work of Interpretation* (Philadelphia: University of Pennsylvania Press, 1983).

30. See, for example, Elizabeth Campbell and Luke Eric Lassiter, "From Collaborative Ethnography to Collaborative Pedagogy: Reflections on the Other Side of Middletown Project and Community-University Research Partnerships," *Anthropology & Education Quarterly*, vol. 41, no. 4 (2010): 370–385; but see esp. Elizabeth Campbell, "Being and Writing with Others: On the Possibilities of an Ethnographic Composition Pedagogy," PhD diss., Indiana University of Pennsylvania, 2011.

31. See Peter Vandenburg, Sue Hum, and Jennifer Clary-Lemon, *Relations, Locations, Positions: Composition Theory for Writing Teachers* (Urbana, IL: National Council of Teachers of English, 2006), 10.

32. Marilyn Cooper, "The Ecology of Writing," *College English*, vol. 48, no. 4 (1986), 373.

33. Campbell, "Being and Writing with Others," 2.

34. See Thomas Deans, *Writing Partnerships: Service-Learning in Composition* (Urbana, IL: National Council of Teachers of English, 2000).

35. Excerpted in part from Campbell, "Being and Writing with Others," 222.

36. Campbell, "Being and Writing with Others," 188.

37. For more on this idea, see Campbell, "Being and Writing with Others."

38. It is also critical to remember that literacies like writing are never neutral or transparent; they are always as tied to social, cultural, and political contexts as they are to practical skills. (Actually, many would argue that they are much more tied to the former than to the latter.) Moreover, literacies are also contested, negotiated, and particular; they are embedded in social systems that dispense both power and powerlessness. What this means, for our purposes, is that we – and here we mean all of those involved in any given project – need to attend as closely as we can to this reality as we create and share our texts.

39. Lassiter, *The Chicago Guide to Collaborative Ethnography*, 139.

Index

action research   24
African American Pioneers Museum
    Exhibition   114–15
American Anthropological Association
    (AAA)   38
    and "Code of Ethics"   38
American Folklore Society (AFS)   38
    and "Position Statement on Research
    with Human Subjects"   38
Amerikaner, Layne   48
anonymity see ethics
Appalachia   35–6
Autoethnography   124

Barz, Gregory   13, 56–7
Behar, Ruth   13, 134
Beudry, Nicole   1
bikers, research on   2, 96, 115
Boas, Franz   58
Bray, John N.   26
Briggs, Charles   87, 94–5, 96, 108

Campbell, Elizabeth   27
Chicago School   58
Clair, Robin Patric   134
Clifford, James   8, 72, 123–4, 134
collaboration
    complexities of   21–6, 34–6, 105–7, 116
    and ethics   39–40
    and reciprocity   32–4
    and working with difference   21–3,
    105–6
    see also fieldwork
collaborative ethnography   6, 7, 9, 11,
    125–6
    and change/transformation   129–34
    see also ethnographic description
communication, channels of   86–7, 104
consultants see ethnography
Cooley, Timothy   13, 56–7
cooperative inquiry see ethnography
critical ethnography   124–5
culture, ideas of   8

Doing Ethnography Today: Theories, Methods, Exercises, First Edition. Elizabeth Campbell
and Luke Eric Lassiter.
© 2015 Elizabeth Campbell and Luke Eric Lassiter. Published 2015 by John Wiley & Sons,
Ltd.

Denzin, Norman 13, 42, 47, 134
dialogic ethnography 124
Doyebi, Ernest 84–5
Du Bois, W. E. B 58

Ellis, Carolyn 124
Ellis, Clyde 84
emergent design 30–47
Emerson, Robert 66, 80
equipment, field *see* fieldwork
ethics, research
  and anonymity/recognition, issues of
    37–41
  codes and statements for 37–40
  and collaboration 39–40
  and field commitments 5–6, 36–40
  and informed consent 36
  and Institutional Review Boards (IRBs)
    39, 41–4, 46
  and interviews 99
ethnographer
  being an 1, 3, 4, 131
  and being a reader, being an 7
  role of 44–6
ethnographic description 66, 72–5
  and collaborative writing 75–7, 129–34
  goals of 128–9
  and making sense of materials 116–20
  and thick description 66–7, 72
  and the writing process 75–7, 133–4
  see also ethnographies
ethnographic interviews *see* interviews
ethnographies
  kinds/forms of 113–16, 120–26
ethnography
  and activism, issues of 102–4, 125–6
  as applied 21–2, 125
  and art 8–13
  authority, issues of 44–7
  as collaborative 5–6, 19–26, 34–6,
    74–7, 103–4
  and consultants/participants 44–6
  as creative and constitutive 7
  and culture 8

defined 1, 4–10
  and dialogue 33–4, 98–104
  and experience 4–5, 10–13, 46–7
  as genre 120–26
  as hermeneutic 6–7
  as partial and emergent 123–4
  as personal 4–5
  as positioned 5
  and qualitative/quantitative methods
    9–10, 34–6, 74–7, 103–4
  and reading 7
  and reflexivity 54–6
  and relationships 5–6, 11, 33, 44–7
  and science 9, 73, 121–2
  and text 6–7
  and writing 7
  see also collaborative ethnography;
    ethics; ethnographer; ethnographies;
    ethnographic description; fieldnotes

Faubion, James D. 27
feminist ethnography 122–3
"The Field" 19–21
  see also fieldwork
Field, Les W. 27
fieldnotes 51–61, 64–79
  approaches to 66–77
  definitions of 66–9
  and experience 51, 54, 69–72
  and inscription/transcription/description
    72–3
  kinds/forms of 67–75
  as mediated 72–5
  and positionality 54–6
  as storied 66–75
fieldwork 2
  and equipment 61–3
  and indexing/coding collected texts
    119
  as multi-sited 20, 58
  and organizing field materials, issues of
    116–20
  and participation, issues of 56–9,
    64–9

fieldwork (*cont'd*)
  as sites of collaboration 15–26
  and virtual ethnography 58
Fluehr-Lobban, Carolyn 45
Foley, Douglas 3
Fretz, Rachel 66, 80

Geertz, Clifford 10, 13, 122, 123
  and thick description 66, 124
Giardina, Michael 42, 47
Goodall, H. L. (Bud) 3, 7
Goodall, Hurley 16–18, 27, 37, 44–5,
  126
Gordon, Deborah A. 134

Hesse-Biber, Sharlene Nagy 48
Hinson, Glenn 10, 101–2, 103
Hurston, Zora Neale 122

Indiana Arts Commission 50
Indiana Historical Society 50, 115
informed consent *see* ethics
Institutional Review Boards (IRBs) *see*
  ethics
interviews 87–9
  as conversations 97–104
  and cooperative action 102–4
  in ethnographic research 89–104
  kinds/forms of 100–104
  legal and ethical concerns involved in
  99
  and participant checking 101, 114
  preparation for 89–94
  procedures for 91–4, 100–104
  as speech events 94–7
  and transcripts 104–8

Johnson, Michelle Natasya 27

Kiowa Indians 20–21, 38, 114
  interviews with 95–6, 99, 100, 101
  and "singings" 85–6, 89
  and song traditions 56, 84–6, 88–9
Kotay, Ralph 84

Lake County Fair Project 50–54, 59–61,
  67, 74, 77–9, 104, 115
Lassiter, Luke Eric 27, 135
Lawless, Elaine 123
Leavy, Patricia 48
Lederman, Rena 66
Lee, Joyce 26
Lincoln, Yvonna S. 13, 134
Lincoln County Girls' Resiliency Program
  (GRP) 35–6
Lindahl, Carl 4
Lynd, Helen Merrell 15, 16, 58
  see also Middletown studies
Lynd, Robert 15, 16, 58
  see also Middletown studies

Malinowski, Bronislaw 57–8, 72–3, 121–3
  and the "native point of view" 57, 73,
  120
  and participant observation 57
Mannheim, Bruce 108
Marcus, George 19, 27, 134
Markham, Annette 100
Mead, Margaret 125
Mesquaki Indians 3
Middletown studies, Lynds' 15, 16, 126–7
Muncie 15–18, 114
  see also Middletown studies; Other Side
  of Middletown Project

Narcotics Anonymous 68, 115
Native American Studies 20–21
Neighborhood Story Project 33, 135

observant participation 64–75
oral history 30–31, 37–8
  and interviews 96–7, 99
Oral History Association (OHA) 37
  and "Principles and Best Practices for
  Oral History" 37–8
Other Side of Middletown Project xi–xii,
  15–18, 31
  and authority, issues of 44–5
  and change/transformation 75, 102, 130

and doing collaborative ethnography
23, 26, 74, 114, 126–8
and negotiated ethical commitments
37, 38
producing ethnographic text   33

Parsons, Elsie Clews   122
participant observation   46–7, 50–61,
64–6
see also observant participation
participation *see* fieldwork
participatory action research   24
postmodern ethnography   123–4
Powers, Willow Roberts   108

qualitative/quantitative research continuum
see ethnography

Rappaport, Joanne   102, 103, 108
reading ethnography   7
see also ethnographies
reciprocity   32–4
see also collaboration
recorders *see* fieldwork
Regional Indigenous Council of Cauca
(CRIC)   102
Remsburg, Rich   50
research *see kinds of*
research ethics *see* ethics, research
research imaginaries   20, 125
research questions, developing   24–6
Rose, Dan   124

Sanjek, Roger   80
Shaw, Linda   66
Smith, Linda L.   26
Spatig, Linda   35–6, 48
Stoller, Paul   120

Tedlock, Barbara   64, 73, 80, 122
and observant participation   64–6
Tedlock, Dennis   108
thick description *see* ethnographic
description
Thomas, Jim   124
Thorp, Laurie   34–5
Traditional Arts Indiana (TAI)   50, 115
Transcripts *see* interviews

Virginia B. Ball Center for Creative Inquiry
(VBC)   17–18, 19
VISTA: Volunteers in Service to America
31

Webb, Beatrice Potter   58
West Virginia   21, 30, 115
activist oral history project in   30–32,
115
university-school study in   21–2, 40–41,
104–5, 114
writing ethnography   133–4
see also ethnographic description

Yorks, Lyle   26
Yow, Valerie   96, 108

Printed and bound by CPI Group (UK) Ltd, Croydon, CR0 4YY

25/03/2025

14647327-0004